The Pride of Phoebus:

The Illustrious History of the Phoebus Fire
Department

Tim Receveur
Tom Jackson

CONTENTS

ACKNOWLEDGMENTS

We would like to thank the past and present firefighters from the Phoebus Fire Company who generously gave us their time to assist with this book. Through their stories and photos, Tony Schmidt, John A. Cizmar, Sr., Hank Beimler, John R. Cooke, Jr., Paul Sulzberger, Don Blagg, and Tom Mugler helped us to understand the structure and the history of the fire department and what the organization has meant to Phoebus over the years.

- Martha Morris for sharing her extensive collection of priceless artifacts from Phoebus and Fort Monroe history.

- Laura Sandford, for letting Robert's Antiques serve as a neighborhood gathering spot for sharing memories, photos, and stories about Phoebus.

- Joe Griffith for his enthusiasm of Phoebus history and for the wonderful illustration in the book.

- Hampton History Museum, especially Seamus McGrann and Beth Austin, for their help in promoting our last Phoebus book and for letting us use several of the photo artifacts in this book.

- The Hampton Public Library, who once again helped immensely with their photo collections, microfiche, and rare books on Phoebus in their Virginia Collection.

- The *Daily Press* for their archives that stretch back into the late 1800s. Without these archives, it is almost impossible to write a book.

- Thank you to everyone who has supported our online efforts. If you haven't seen them, please visit our daily blog *Phoebus and Fort Monroe: Then and Now* on Facebook and Instagram and our community website *Phoebus Memories* (phoebusmemories.org) where you can find many of the photos and stories from this book.

Like Phoebus, the Phoebus Fire Department has had many names over the years. It was called The Phoebus Hook and Ladder Company No. 1 on its inception, followed simply by Phoebus Fire Department, and the Phoebus Fire Company after consolidation with Hampton. We use the names interchangeably in the book.

"We of the present Hampton, we who love this old place either because it is our home by inheritance or adoption must carry on and remember that we are its guardians and makers and that the Hampton of the future will be the sort of place we are making it today."

- Bessie Lee Booker (1922)

"In this world in which we live, either we go ahead or go backwards. Some people and some organizations are content to live in the past and to spend their time recalling memories and events of years ago. But not so with the Phoebus Fire Department."

- Judge Percy Carmel (1938)

FOREWORD

There is a well know mantra in the modern fire service that goes something like the most dangerous phrase in the fire service is *"we've always done it that way."* I've even seen it painted on walls in firehouses. It's intended to be a warning against complacency and to spark quality improvement. Another goes "The American Fire Service, 100 years of tradition unimpeded by progress." Both were no doubt conceived either on the front bumper of a firetruck or around a firehouse kitchen table, where all of the problems of the fire department (and the world as a whole) have been solved thousands of times over. I would offer tradition perhaps deserves a second look. Many traditions were ill-conceived and abhorrent but others fostered tremendous teamwork, an appreciation of family, and pride in one's community.

As you read this book, you will begin to meet and hopefully understand some of the men who (unknowingly) constructed the romantic image we attribute to firemen. I have been in the fire service for almost 35 years and I can count on one hand the number of times where I was really in fear for my life. Gone are the days where the dirtier or bloodier you were, the cooler you were. Gone are the days when bravery was a synonym for reckless or unsafe. The world was not the same, Phoebus was not the same, and society was not the same. Please be cautious not to apply today's values to the Phoebus of a century ago. We still have the little wooden box with a ½ inch hole in the top that every member put either a white or black marble (ball) in to vote. Back when this was a small town, everybody knew everyone else and if a member of the Company didn't want you in, they just "black balled" you. Right or wrong, reason or not… that's how it worked. Today, we have physical agility tests, and background checks and even polygraphs for our new volunteers. In the end, who's to say which system is more effective?

Yes, the modern fire service has changed drastically and that is a wonderful thing. Gone are the days when ability to drive a truck fast and run a pump were all that was needed to make for a good recruit. Today we have computer in the cab for the officer, and ballistic vests to protect us in case someone starts shooting at us. We have cardiac monitors that rival what is in the ICU and a box full of drugs and firefighters with training and experience to use them to save lives. Many years ago, "lantern boys" were young men who learned the skills of firefighting by watching and training with their fathers, uncles, men they looked up to. That was a good system for its time. A ride in the Cadillac ambulance across town to Dixie Hospital saved many lives. It's not fair to say that civic pride has dwindled or that there is not enough desire to help one's neighbor, we have simply evolved to a point where the demands are more than most are willing to bear. We still offer pride and status and a sense of belonging. Gone too are the parades, and the camaraderie that came from traveling to compete in the Virginia State Firefighters Convention and sleeping in a tent.

We have made incredible progress but, perhaps there are certain customs/traits/characteristics of the past that we do not want to leave behind. My challenge for you, as you read *The Pride of Phoebus,* is to find as many of the beneficial traditions from the Phoebus Fire Company and help us to keep them alive for the future firefighters, whomever they be.

John R. Cooke, Jr.
Chief, Phoebus Volunteer Fire Company

KEY PHOEBUS FIRE DEPARTMENT DATES

1893	Huge fire at Mellen and Mallory Streets leads to the creation of The Phoebus Hook and Ladder Company No. 1. P.A. Fuller elected as First Chief
1893	Firemen's Hall built by P.A. Fuller on land donated by the Lancer family. Construction took two months and cost $694.
1898	Riots in Phoebus
1898	George H. Lancer elected as 2nd Fire Chief
1899	Yellow fever outbreak and quarantine
1900	Town (formerly Chesapeake City) incorporated and renamed Phoebus
1901	Fuller's restaurant and hotel opens (by former Chief Fuller)
1905	Massive fire on Mellen and Mallory Street
1912	John Ferber elected as 3rd Fire Chief
1917	Frank A. Kearney elected as 4th Fire Chief
1918	Spanish Flu outbreak. Chief Frank A. Kearney dies
1918	George H. Lancer re-elected as 5th Fire Chief
1920	Chamberlin Hotel fire
1930	Phoebus hosts the Virginia State Firemen's Association annual convention
1931	Anton Alexander Schmidt elected as 6th Fire Chief
1938	New Fire Department and Town Hall built for $35,500
1948	The Phoebus Volunteer Rescue Squad forms
1952	Phoebus consolidates with the city of Hampton. Phoebus Fire Department renamed Phoebus Volunteer Fire Company
1952	The Phoebus Fire Company Ladies' Auxiliary forms
1953	Phoebus hosts the Virginia State Firemen's Association annual convention
1963	Long-time Fire Chief Schmidt passes away. Robert F. Snow, Jr. elected as 7th Fire Chief
1985	Roseland Manor fire
1993	Phoebus Fire Company celebrates its 100th anniversary
1995	Slaughter Lumber Company fire
2000	Massive renovations and updates to the Phoebus fire station

1 THE FOUNDATION:
1893-1897

In an interview in 1979, Nelson Fuller said that the two most important organizations that bind Phoebus are the Phoebus Volunteer Fire Company and the Phoebus First Aid Squad.[1] For over 125 years, generations of families have served Phoebus with familiar names like Lancer, Snow, Mugler, Carmel, Norman, Hale, Clarke, Carpenters, Turner, Furness, Mittelmaier, Craigs, Hellman, Kaiser, Sharf, Haas, Stowell, Schmidt, Fuller, Sulzberger, Kearney, Selby, Beimler, Loughran, Smith, Larrabee, Kraft, Lewis, Mingee, Hellman, Saunders, and so many more.

A - Fire and EMS recruits in front of the Fire Department on June 12, 2019 (April Receveur).

In its earliest days, Phoebus was a community of tightly packed wooden saloons and houses. Saving the town from burning to ashes would have been enough for most firemen during this time, but the Phoebus Fire Department would be called on to do much more.

They would play a major role in keeping the town from being destroyed

---

[1] Jim Wright, "Phoebus Keeps Best of Past with Today's Changes," *Daily Press* (October 14, 1979).

when a series of riots threatened it in the late 19th and early 20th century. And the Phoebus Fire Department had its "finest moment" when Yellow Fever forced authorities to quarantine the town in 1899.

In the 20th century, the Phoebus Fire Department would witness the greatest changes in the history of firefighting as horses and buckets would be quickly replaced by fire trucks, new pump and ladder technology, and protective gear. Even the horses would resist these incredible changes as you will see.

No member of the Phoebus Fire Department embodied this rapid change more than Anton Alexander (A.A.) Schmidt. Known as Tony, Schmidt started his career as a lamp boy lighting gas lamps around Phoebus in 1905. He would go on to be the Chief of the fire department for three decades and when he died in 1963, he was working in the woodworking department at NASA to help get Americans to the moon.

B - Phoebus lamp boys in 1905. Future Chief A.A. Schmidt is in the middle standing (Tony Schmidt).

Charles H. Warren of Phoebus joined the Phoebus Fire Company in 1893 and never missed a convention or a parade. He was interviewed in 1956 after 63 years of fighting fires and said, "a hand pump, some hose and bucket, mounted on a horse-drawn carriage, was the only equipment available to the Phoebus Company in its early years." However, he said that it was much "more fun fighting fires in the old days."[2]

Today, the Phoebus Station is supported by three platoons of career fire and rescue personnel. The Phoebus district includes Hampton University, the Veterans Administration Medical Center, historic Fort Monroe, Interstate 64, and the Hampton Roads Bridge Tunnel.

C - In Memoriam – List of Phoebus Firefighters, Ladies' Auxiliary, and First Aid Squad members who have passed in the Phoebus Fire Company (Tim Receveur).

The Beginning: Fire and Ice

The Phoebus Hook and Ladder Company No. 1, as it was officially known in the beginning, got its start in the middle of a blizzard. A massive winter storm went through the Peninsula, dropping more than a foot of snow on the night of January 19, 1893.

Looking down Mellen Street today, it's not that hard to imagine that Phoebus was tightly-packed with blocks and blocks of wood buildings. With no modern insulation and with temperatures plummeting, fires were heating homes and saloons around town. In those days, many saloons were open 24 hours a day. Details are scarce, but in the middle of the

---

[2] "Oldest Volunteer in Parade Today," *Daily Press* (August 17, 1956).

snowstorm, a fire broke out near the intersection of Mellen and Mallory Streets around 3am and it roared uncontrollably until the late morning.

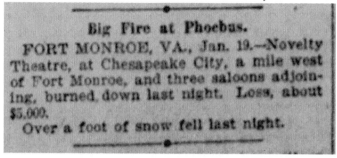

Big Fire at Phoebus.

FORT MONROE, VA., Jan. 19.—Novelty Theatre, at Chesapeake City, a mile west of Fort Monroe, and three saloons adjoining, burned down last night. Loss, about $5,000.

Over a foot of snow fell last night.

D - Article from The Times (Richmond, Virginia), January 20, 1893

By the time it was finished, the fire would destroy the Novelty Theatre, Fitzgerald's and Hodges' saloons, William's Restaurant, the town stables, and 100 cords of wood at Tennis and Topping.[3] Phoebus would be forever transformed. *The Times* (Richmond) wrote that "nothing but a miracle saved the town. Harder work was never done to extinguish the fire."[4]

E - Tennis and Topping Building at 11 East Mellen Street around 1890.

---

[3] 100 cords of wood which would measure 400 feet x 400 feet x 800 feet.
[4] "The Fire in Phoebus," *The Times (Richmond, Virginia)* (January 21, 1893).

The fear of what happened would lead the citizens of the devastated town to take some drastic action. Less than a week later the Phoebus Fire Department formed on January 25, 1893.

Today it is called the Phoebus Volunteer Fire Company, and the Phoebus station was designated as Hampton Fire Department Station 2 when Phoebus consolidated with Hampton in 1952. It is the second oldest company in the city after the Hampton Fire Department which got its start in 1884, after an even bigger disaster.[5]

A devastating fire in April 1884 burned nearly half of downtown Hampton and it would take a united effort from firefighters from the Hampton, Phoebus, and Fort Monroe areas to save the other half.[6] The destruction resulted in the formation of the Hampton Volunteer Fire Company.

> THE CONFLAGRATION AT HAMPTON. VA.—The fair little town of Hampton, has been visited by a conflagration which swept away the most of its business section. The fire broke out at three o'clock Wednesday morning, and owing to the high wind spread rapidly. Engines from the Normal School, the Soldiers' Home and Fort Monroe were sent for, and by their united efforts saved half the town from destruction. Thirty buildings, mostly frame, occupied as stores and dwellings, were consumed.— The estimated loss is $100,000.

Headlines from the fire in Hampton (*Staunton Spectator*).

One of the heroes battling the fire in Hampton was Richard A. Ruth, Sr., a Union veteran who was captured at the Battle of Cold Harbor during the Civil War and was imprisoned as a POW at Libby Prison in the

---

[5] "History of the Phoebus Volunteer Fire Department" *Phoebus Volunteer Fire Department* (2019), 3.

[6] "The Conflagration at Hampton," *The Staunton Spectator* (April 15, 1884).

Confederate capital of Richmond. He would be in and out of military hospitals after the war and came to the Old Soldiers' Home near Phoebus in 1873. Ruth was part of the firefighting unit from the Old Soldiers' Home.

F - Richard A. Ruth, Sr., one of the heroes of the "Great Fire" in Hampton in 1884 and a charter member of the Phoebus Fire Department in 1893 (John Ruth).

Hampton leaders gave Ruth a commemorative badge for his efforts to save Hampton during the "Great Fire" in 1884. Engraved on reverse side: "Presented to Richard A. Ruth by the Citizens of Hampton Va. as a testimonial of their appreciation of his noble efforts to save the town from destruction at the fire of April 9th, 1884."

Ruth would also become a charter member of the Phoebus Fire Department in 1893. In the minutes from one of its earliest meetings, the Phoebus Fire Department minutes say that "it is ordered that Dick Ruth be tendered an honorary life membership."[7]

Historic Phoebus

Phoebus is only one-mile square in size, but it has had an oversized share of history. Through the years, Phoebus has played host to railroads and streetcars, the first community for slaves seeking freedom in the South, soldiers from Fort Monroe, Civil War veterans, a century of vacationers, and more saloons per capita than any other place in the United States in its early days (at least that we could find).

Phoebus would also be home to the Kecoughtan Indians when the first English explorers landed on their way to Jamestown in 1607. Later, numerous Virginia Governors and U.S. Presidents like Abraham Lincoln would pay visits. President John Tyler would even have a villa in the Phoebus area.[8] Historical figures and celebrities like Harriet Tubman, Booker T. Washington, Minnesota Fats, Ella Fitzgerald, Duke Ellington, and reportedly even gangsters Al Capone and "Baby Face" Nelson have also made their way through Phoebus through the decades.

Phoebus has always been a progressive and entrepreneurial town. The Hampton Monitor in 1907 described Phoebus as "the most cosmopolitan little city where people from all backgrounds, nationalities and creeds live in harmony" adding that social standing in the community is "earned by brains, common sense and civic interest rather than by family background."[9] This would be embodied in 1901, the year of its first election, where William H. Trusty and N.C. Barnes were elected to the

---

[7] Phoebus Fire Department Meeting Minutes, (February 20, 1893).

[8] Anne W. Chapman, "Fight For Home Saves Plantation," *Daily Press* (August 11, 1991).

[9] Annie C. Newsome, "The Phoebus Story - Past and Present," *Daily Press* (December 7, 1969).

Town Council. They were two of the earliest African-American elected officials in the state of Virginia.[10] It would also be apparent when local church congregations vocally opposed slavery before the Civil War.[11]

Phoebus has persevered when war came to its shores, most notably during the Civil War. Phoebus would be the location of the first Union Army camp in Virginia after succession. The town would be at the center of mobilization efforts during the Spanish-American War and World War I. Phoebus would be on edge when it was quarantined for yellow fever in 1899 and would be hit hard during the global scourge of Spanish Flu in 1918 where it tragically took the life of the Chief of the fire department.[12]

When the Phoebus Hook and Ladder Company No. 1 officially began on January 25, 1893 in Kaiser's Hall, the town was still officially referred to as Chesapeake City even though it was starting to be called Phoebus regularly.

Harrison Phoebus

The name Phoebus would come from Harrison Phoebus, a Civil War veteran from Maryland who came to Fort Monroe in 1866. Phoebus became a "one-man industry" serving as Old Point Comfort's "postmaster, notary public, U.S. commissioner, insurance agent, and representative of shipping companies."[13]

Phoebus would be put in charge of the Hygeia Hotel at Fort Monroe in 1873 and he would turn it into one of the most magnificent hotels during the Victorian Age. He would later convince railroad tycoon Collis P.

---

[10] National Registry of Historic Places, "William H. Trusty House," *United States Department of the Interior* (United States: June 22, 1979), https://www.dhr.virginia.gov/VLR_to_transfer/PDFNoms/114-0108_WillamHTrustyHouse_1979_Final_Nomination.pdf.

[11] Dave Schleck, "Phoebus United Methodist Began As A 'Yankee Church'," *Daily Press* (December 8, 1995).

[1212] "Frank A. Kearney Dies in Phoebus from Influenza," *Daily Press* (October 24, 1918).

[13] Parke Rouse, Jr, *The Good Old Days in Hampton and Newport News* (USA: Dietz Press, 1986), 67.

Huntington to extend the tracks of the Chesapeake and Ohio Railroad (C&O) to Chesapeake City by the end of 1882 and later to Fort Monroe in 1890.[14]

Chesapeake City would name the rail station Phoebus in his honor in 1882. Later the post office would be renamed as well and many newspaper articles at this time started referring to Chesapeake City as Phoebus and the name stuck. It would take until April 2, 1900 to make it official. Phoebus died suddenly of a heart ailment on February 25, 1886 at the age of 45, but he made a lasting impact in the community that still bears his name.

G - C&O train on the turntable in Phoebus in 1940 (Photo courtesy of the C&O Historical Society - http://cohs.org).

The Charter Members

At the first meeting of the Phoebus Fire Department in Kaiser's Hall on January 25, 1893, 33 members of the community became charter members and membership was extended until March 1.[15] Phillip A. (P.A.) Fuller was named the first fire chief, with Edward C. (E.C.) Kaiser, Sr, foreman, Joseph Went, secretary, and L.G. Donohue, treasurer. Records of the department show that $210 subscribed by charter members was the only initial financial support available to the company. This money bought a

---

[14] "Peninsula Extension," *Wikipedia* (March 21, 2018), https://en.wikipedia.org/wiki/Peninsula_Extension.
[15] Phoebus Fire Department Meeting Minutes, (January 25, 1893).

hand pump, hose, and a few buckets.[16]

H - The original fire station around 1897 before the addition of the bell tower. Mellen Street is off in the distance (Tom Jackson photo).

During the first year the members were called upon to contribute funds and to solicit from other sources to purchase fire equipment, uniforms for department members, and other necessary apparatus.[17] Town leaders promised future funds via tax revenues, but the "need to protect the community was tantamount" and the "officers and members realized the need for more adequate and state-of-the-art firefighting equipment."[18]

Duty of the finance committee, as recorded in the first minutes, was "to solicit contributions from the public generally for the purpose of buying such fire apparatus as may be designated by this body." After intensive fundraising in the community, the fledgling Fire Company members authorized the purchase of a hand drawn Hook and Ladder wagon. The Hook and Ladder Truck No. 1 was listed as Figure 333 of Rumsey's

---

[16] "Phoebus Volunteers Began Fire Fighting Unit in '93," *Daily Press* (July 12, 1953).
[17] "New Town Fire Department Culminates Dream Fostered 40 Years Ago in Phoebus," *Daily Press* (November 20, 1938).
[18] "History of the Phoebus Volunteer Fire Department" *Phoebus Volunteer Fire Department* (2019), 3.

Catalogue for $438.75.[19]

The Fire Company asked the community to name the new wagon. Names like "Rescue," "Citizen's Gift," and "Hustler" were proposed. After what the meeting minutes describe as a "lively discussion," the members voted unanimously to name their first apparatus "Citizen's Gift."[20] It would get a workout over the next few years. It was also agreed that the Fire Department would meet weekly on Mondays at 8pm.[21]

I - Charter Members of the Phoebus Fire Department from January 25, 1893 (Phoebus Fire Department).

At the first regular meeting on January 30, 1893, complete organization of the company effected the newly elected officers as Chief, P.A. Fuller; Foreman, E.C. Kaiser, Sr.; Secretary; Joseph Went; and Treasurer L.G. Donohue; and

With them the following citizens were made charter members: P.H. Boyhan, P.W. Phillips, Joseph Daly, E.M. Tennis, W.F. Clarke, J.B. Fairchild, W.J. Kearney, George H. Lancer, A. Killmeyer, F. Probst, S.T. Larcomb, Ollie Freeburger, Lewis Prentiss, Stephen Cony, J.J. Shean, William Fuller, A.C. Lacy, Edward Farrell, W.H. Power who became secretary at that meeting. Thomas A. Stacey, Frank Lancer, P. Detroit, L. Bradley, J.W. Opdyke, C.A.

---

[19] Phoebus Fire Department Meeting Minutes, (February 20, 1893).
[20] "History of the Phoebus Volunteer Fire Department" *Phoebus Volunteer Fire Department* (2019), 3.
[21] Phoebus Fire Department Meeting Minutes, (January 30, 1893).

Eacho, H.S. Kelly, George Young, Charles Wornom, and W.H. Larrabee.

The Fire Station

The original fire station was built in 1893 on land donated to the Phoebus Fire Department by the Lancer family. The first Fire Chief, P.A. Fuller was a highly-respected architect in the region and was chosen to construct the new building.

Fuller received the contract to build the fire station on April 13, 1893[22] for $694. It was built in only two months and opened on June 12, 1893.[23]

Fireman's Hall as it was called stood steadfastly until it was replaced with the current building in 1938. Fireman's Hall had many modifications over its 45-year history including the addition of a bell tower, horse stables, and hay lofts for the horses, which pulled the steamer engines.

J - With the additional stables to the right around 1898 (Tom Jackson).

The Fire Department would hold a large fair in Phoebus later that summer on July 11-13, 1893 to raise more funds. According to receipts from July 17,

---

[22] Phoebus Fire Department Meeting Minutes, (April 13, 1893).
[23] Phoebus Fire Department Meeting Minutes, (June 12, 1893).

they raised $613.88.[24] These funds purchased "four dozen buckets, a half dozen axes, three dozen chairs," and all new hats, coats, and shirts."[25]

At the first meeting after the fair on July 31, 1893, E.C. Kaiser asked for permission to use the Church bell in case of a fire and on special occasions.

It was approved and a dozen keys were purchased for the chuck doors. The Fire Department also voted to raffle the leftover cake from the Fair on August 1.[26] It probably wasn't the freshest after more than two weeks.

K - Phoebus Hook and Ladder Company No. 1 with the new bell tower in 1899 (Tom Jackson photo).

---

[24] Phoebus Fire Department Meeting Minutes, (July 17, 1893).
[25] Phoebus Fire Department Meeting Minutes, (July 24, 1893).
[26] Phoebus Fire Department Meeting Minutes, (July 31, 1893).

L - Phoebus Fire Department in 1899 (Tom Jackson).

| **Pride of Phoebus Spotlight**
Phillip A. Fuller
First Phoebus Fire Chief
Life: 1860 – 1916

Phillip A. Fuller was known to the community as P.A. Fuller. Fuller was selected as the first Fire Chief of the Phoebus Fire Department and also built the original fire station in 1893. It served the community faithfully until it was removed to make way for the current building in 1938.

Fuller was a noted architect and builder on the Lower Peninsula who built many of the Victorian homes throughout Phoebus and Hampton in the late 1800s and early 1900s. This includes the Queen Anne style residence of William H. Trusty in 1897 which still survives on County Street. Trusty was one of the first African-Americans elected in a municipality in Virginia and the house P.A. Fuller built for him was called "the nicest house in Phoebus" when it was completed.

During the Jamestown Exposition in 1907, a local publication described Fuller as an "up-to-date hotel man who had not done anything by halves to prepare for the exposition." Today Fuller is known best for building and running Fuller's Restaurant and Hotel. Fuller's opened in 1901 and was run by three generations of the family and was a Phoebus treasure before it finally closed in 1989.

M -Fire helmet worn by P.A. Fuller - with permission of the Phoebus Fire Company (Courtesy of the Hampton History Museum -ID #: L2003.21.1)

N - P.A. Fuller in full uniform around 1897 (Tom Jackson).

2 RIOTS AND QUARANTINE:
1898-1899

The end of the century would be an exceptionally rough period for the Phoebus Fire Department. The events that would transpire from 1898-1900 would become legendary and would galvanize the Fire Department and make them even more revered in the community.

Mallory and County Streets were once a center for businesses in Phoebus at the end of the 19th century. The area that included a large section of Mallory Street was called Slabtown and it was the first community for freed slaves in the South during the Civil War.[27]

African-American entrepreneurship thrived during this time in Phoebus with many owning restaurants, hotels, and saloons. One of the most successful in the late 1800s was Norfleet C. Barnes. Known by the community as N.C. Barnes, he would become a member of the Phoebus Town Council in its first election in 1901.

This is how the *Phoebus Sentinel* covered his election in 1901: "N.C. Barnes has lived in Phoebus for the past thirty years and is well-known throughout the country. He established his present business at Barnes' Corner in 1886 and has conducted it successfully ever since. He is a large property owner and well-liked and respected by all classes. He will no doubt represent the Fifth Ward with credit."[28]

Annie Jones and her family were renting a house from Barnes at the intersection of County and Fulton Streets in 1898. On the night of September 27, 1898, Annie turned down her kerosene lamp to low and went to bed. Around midnight, Annie awoke to see her husband screaming that their house was on fire!

Annie quickly pulled her two small children out of bed, but she still needed to wake her older son in another room. The door was locked and it took

---

[27] John V. Quarstein (historian, *Big Bethel: The First Battle*), conversation with author, January 9, 2019.
[28] "The New Town Councilmen," *Phoebus Sentinel* (July 6, 1901).

nearly two minutes to wake him. This left her with barely enough time to get down the stairs and safely outside. In the confusion, an onlooker feared the older son might still be inside the raging inferno and he ran upstairs just as the stairs collapsed. He would be forced to flee the flames by jumping out the 2nd story window.[29]

STOCK.

A strong northwest wind was blowing while the Jones building was burning, and it is said that but for the prompt response and cool work of the Phoebus fire department an extensive conflagration could not have been prevented. The flames were blown underneath Barnes' house and set fire to the weather-boarding on the other side.

O - Article referring to the events of September 27, 1898 (Daily Press).

By this time, the Phoebus Fire Department had arrived. Strong northwest winds were blowing the fire towards heavily populated Barnes' Corner which included the house and saloon owned by Barnes. The *Daily Press* reported "but for the prompt response and cool work of the Phoebus fire department, an extensive conflagration could not have been prevented." The Jones family would lose everything in the fire, but they reported that they felt very lucky to have escaped with their lives.[30]

Earlier that year, an old Civil War veteran would not be so lucky.

Old Soldiers Home

A history of Phoebus would be incomplete without discussing the Old Soldiers Home which was known officially as the Southern Branch of the National Home for Disabled Volunteer Soldiers. The Old Soldiers Home was established in 1870 on the southwest corner of Phoebus and treated thousands of Civil War veterans over more than 75 years. The facility is called the Hampton VA Center today.

In the late 1800s it was common in Phoebus to see hundreds of Civil War

---

[29] "The Lamp Exploded," *Daily Press* (September 28, 1898).
[30] Ibid.

veterans each day and the saloons in town operated 24 hours a day to accommodate their pensions.

On March 26, 1898 a fire broke out at the aptly named Half-Way House, a saloon which was located on Mallory Street, half-way between the Old Soldiers Home and Mellen Street. The establishment served alcohol on the 1st floor and provided beds on the 2nd floor for the veterans who stayed out after their curfew.

A fire broke out upstairs around 3:30am where several old soldiers were reportedly sleeping. James Duncan was startled awake and at once sounded the alarm. He woke up old soldier John Ingered who panicked. Duncan tried to get him to come to his senses but failed. The fire company of Phoebus responded to the alarm promptly, but there were no water plugs in the vicinity, and it was impossible to use the hoses.

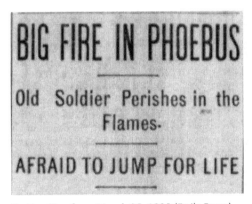

P - Headline from March 26, 1898 (Daily Press).

Duncan jumped from the second story to safety as did several other veterans. Ingered took too long and was overwhelmed by the smoke and flames and sadly died.[31]

The fire soon spread to the house adjoining the saloon, and in a few minutes it was at the mercy of the flames. It then looked as if the fire would spread still further, and the third house commenced to burn, and "had it not pulled down before the flames had gotten control there's no telling when the fire may have been extinguished."[32]

As it would turn out, these fires would be a precursor to huge events in 1898 that would rock Phoebus that year. The town would be lucky to survive the next few months.

Old soldiers would continue to be a fixture in Phoebus for many decades more, but young soldiers would play a much greater role in Phoebus as the

---

[31] "Big Fire in Phoebus," *Daily Press* (March 26, 1898).
[32] Ibid.

Spanish American War began in April 1898.

Phoebus Saloons

"Drunkenness, rioting, fighting and gambling are the order of the day. One businessman told me that on such days, there was 'a fight every five minutes.' He stated that frequently he could stand at the door of his place and see 'three or four fights going on at once.'"[33] - June 1898

When early Phoebus is mentioned, the first thought that many people have is one of saloons running the length of Mallory and Mellen Streets and its later reputation as "Little Chicago" for the excessive drinking, gambling, and fighting that went on in the late 19th and early 20th century.

In 1898, the *Daily Press* mentions that there were "63 saloons running at full blast" in Phoebus.[34] Some unofficial publications put the number as high as 83. Regardless of the exact number, Phoebus had one of the highest concentrations of saloons per capita in the world for a town that was roughly 1 mile by 1 mile in size.

One publication called Phoebus "the most dangerous port on the Atlantic seaboard."[35]

Riots in Phoebus

"There has been a deep love affair between Phoebus and Fort Monroe for at least a hundred years, but the course of love is not always smooth."[36] - October 1979

Judging from old newspaper clips and local stories, the highest number of saloons and the worst violence in Phoebus coincided with the Spanish-American War in 1898. Fort Monroe was a major player in the war efforts, and it was the site of thousands of soldiers disembarking and returning from the war.

---

[33] "A Drive at Phoebus," *Daily Press* (June 12, 1898).

[34] Ibid.

[35] Parke Rouse, "Prohibition, Consolidation Unable to Conquer Phoebus," *Daily Press* (February 12, 1995), https://www.dailypress.com/news/dp-xpm-19950212-1995-02-12-9502100251-story.html.

[36] Jim Wright, "Phoebus Keeps Best of Past with Today's Changes," *Daily Press* (October 14, 1979).

Three of the most infamous riots in Phoebus' history came just months apart in 1898 and the Phoebus Fire Department would play a major role in making sure that Phoebus wasn't burned to the ground.

Q - Shore leave at Fort Monroe just one mile from Phoebus (Postcard from personal collection).

June 1898

The first riot took place in June 1898 and it had little to do with the Phoebus Fire Department, but it's good context for what comes next.

The First Regiment Maryland Volunteer Regiment was a unit stationed at Fort Monroe and it would be a constant headache for Phoebus throughout 1898. Around midnight on the night of Tuesday, June 14, an insult would turn into an epic bar fight with 300 soldiers fighting in the streets of Phoebus.[37]

The Maryland volunteers would start throwing punches when regulars at Fort Monroe insulted their "military training" and their state. Phoebus authorities were "unable to quell the disturbance" and asked Fort Monroe for help.[38] Colonel William P. Lane, who was the commander at Fort Monroe, sent troops who joined with volunteers in Phoebus to stop the

---

[37] "A Disgraceful Riot," *Alexandria Gazette* (June 15, 1898).
[38] Ibid.

fighting. 75 soldiers would be arrested and returned to Fort Monroe to face charges. For the next several weeks, tensions would continue to build between Fort Monroe and Phoebus.[39]

August 1898

The Phoebus Fire Department played a major role in a second riot that took place on August 22-23, 1898. What started with a shooting at George Tucker's "Step Inn" saloon on Mellen Street on August 22, would end with First Regiment Maryland Volunteer Infantry and Colonel Lane forced to leave Fort Monroe.

On Sunday, August 22, reports say that sailors and soldiers had been drinking too much at the saloon when Tucker tried to stop serving them. This angered J.J. Corcoran, a Marine on the collider "Cassius" with the nickname Buffalo.[40] He allegedly struck Tucker and Tucker "whipped out his revolver and shot the man in the leg."[41] Fearing for his life, Tucker kept the other sailors and soldiers at bay with his gun until the police arrived to take him into custody for the shooting.[42] Police had a hard time getting him out of the saloon and many military men made threats on Tucker's life. By this time, more than 1,000 citizens gathered at the scene.[43]

After the police left, Phoebus was the scene of another "riotous disturbance" with "more than a hundred soldiers and sailors wreaking vengeance on the stock of a saloon-keeper". They started by breaking Tucker's glass window with beer barrels, demolishing all the furniture, and throwing out all the bottles of alcohol into the street. They set the saloon on fire by overturning a gasoline stove, but it was extinguished by bystanders. There would be a second attack on the saloon that night when Corcoran's shipmates planned on burning "Step Inn" to the ground. They decided against the plan when they found out he didn't own the building.[44]

Things would get worse on Monday, August 23. Fights took place all day "between sailors and soldiers, who it is said, although fighting among themselves had jointly spotted several saloons for demolition, declaring that

---

[39] "A Disgraceful Riot," *Alexandria Gazette* (June 15, 1898).
[40] "Quiet Restored," *The Times (Richmond)* (August 23, 1898).
[41] "Disorderly Proceedings," *Alexandria Gazette* (August 22, 1898).
[42] "Tucker in Hampton," *Daily Press* (August 24, 1898).
[43] "Disorderly Proceedings," *Alexandria Gazette* (August 22, 1898).
[44] "Quiet Restored," *The Times (Richmond)* (August 23, 1898).

the proprietors had used 'knock-out' drops in order to rob them."[45] At 4pm that afternoon, Phoebus Sheriff Curtis and police officers from Hampton showed up to restore order and arrested four members of the First Regiment Maryland Volunteer Infantry from Fort Monroe. The news quickly spread to soldiers at Fort Monroe that "their comrades had fallen into the hands of civilian authorities" and "by 8 o'clock a large crowd of soldiers had gathered in Phoebus for the purpose of liberating the prisoners."[46]

Sheriff Curtis scrambled and deputized a "score of men" as special constables to "confront the soldier-mob." The new deputies were a mix of white and black citizens including a contingent from the Phoebus Fire Department.

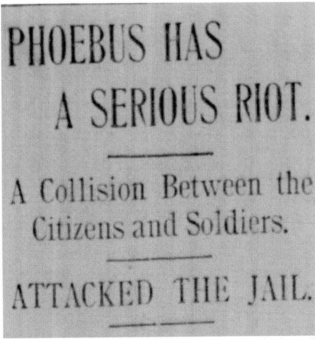

R - Phoebus headlines on August 23, 1898 – The Times (Richmond)

The soldiers arrived and were "courteously asked to leave but declined to do so unless the prisoners could walk out. A one-sided parley ensued, the soldiers at times becoming wildly demonstrative."[47] One report even said

---

[45] "A Riot in Phoebus," *Daily Press* (August 23, 1898).
[46] Ibid.
[47] "Tucker in Hampton," *Daily Press* (August 24, 1898).

the soldiers brought a battering ram to help with the prison break.

The soldiers rushed the jail, firing shots at the officers. Sheriff Curtis gave his men the order to fire. The sheriff's force opened fire: shooting low and hitting nine soldiers.[48] One of the new deputies, Red Hunt, "couldn't be bothered with guns" and "tore off a fence railing and whaled" on one of the soldiers and they "fled from his fury." None of the deputies were injured.[49] "Enough shots were fired in Phoebus tonight to kill fifty men, but fortunately, no one was fatally wounded."[50]

S - Phoebus Fire Company No.1 around 1899. Several of these men help quell the riots in August 1898 (Phoebus Volunteer Fire Company).

---

[48] "Tucker in Hampton," *Daily Press* (August 24, 1898).
[49] "A Riot in Phoebus," *Richmond Dispatch* (August 23, 1898).
[50] Ibid.

"The fire-bell began clanging shortly after the row at the jail began, and that seemed to serve as a signal to the saloonmen to close their places."[51]

On their way back to Fort Monroe the angry soldiers confronted and opened fire on a group of young African-American boys in Phoebus, shooting Charles Smith through the thigh.[52] The vindictive soldiers threatened to kill every man, woman, and child in Phoebus. The situation became so tense that the Mayor sent a telegram to Colonel Lane, commander of Fort Monroe, holding him personally responsible if anything happened. Lane sent 200 soldiers from Company B to Phoebus around 10pm to help restore order.[53] They were scattered across town and at "11 o'clock comparative order had been restored." "Every saloon in the place was closed, and but for the crowds on the streets, Phoebus was a most desolate-looking place."[54]

The Maryland soldiers gave interviews the next day trying to explain their point of view. One of their complaints was that African-Americans were united with Phoebus saloon owners against them.[55] "The soldiers say that they have been badly treated by the Phoebus saloon men and declare that they intend to even up with them. They also claim that the negroes have taken sides with the saloon men against them and hence they have added another score to the account which they say they intend to settle before they get through at Phoebus."[56] The reason for the unity in Phoebus might be that several African-Americans owned their own saloons in town, like future town councilmen William H. Trusty and N.C. Barnes.

The greater sin in the eyes of the soldiers, however, was the fact that Phoebus had deputized African-Americans during the chaos. "The

---

[51] "A Riot in Phoebus," *Richmond Dispatch* (August 23, 1898).
[52] "Ibid.
[53] "Quiet Restored," *The Times (Richmond)* (August 23, 1898).
[54] "A Riot in Phoebus," *Richmond Dispatch* (August 23, 1898).
[55] "Tucker in Hampton," *Daily Press* (August 24, 1898).
[56] Ibid.

Maryland volunteers say that among deputies that fired on them in the skirmish at the jail were a number of negroes and claim that but for the fact that colored deputies were sworn in, there would have been no trouble."[57]

A letter on August 24, 1898 from the First Maryland Volunteer Regiment to the *Daily Press*: "We the soldiers of the First Maryland volunteer regiment, regret that such a disturbance as that which occurred at Phoebus on Monday night, should have taken place between the people and the soldiers, but had the sheriff shown better judgement, or his deputy shown better judgement, than to deputize negroes to shoot at white men there would have been no trouble. For it makes no difference what the men may be, they will not allow a negro to shoot at them as though he was shooting a dog. A dozen white men of the proper class could have subdued all the soldiers who were in Phoebus that night. A word of warning, and not as a threat to the sheriff, let him not put negro policemen on duty in the future to try and arrest or shoot at soldiers for, as we all know, there is a limit to all things. The part the negro took in Monday night's disturbance will not be forgotten by the men of the First Maryland."[58]

Colonel Lane received a message from the Secretary of War that day calling for all soldiers to leave Phoebus and return to post. The saloon owner, George Tucker, who had initially fired on the soldier, was still being held in the Hampton jail. Twenty-five men were deputized and given Winchester rifles to guard him.[59]

Reports from Thursday, August 25, 1898 say that Phoebus had been calm since the arrival of Fort Monroe soldiers on Monday night. The Maryland soldiers involved in the riots would soon be "mustered out of the service," and Colonel Lane would be replaced as commander of Fort Monroe.[60]

October 1898

The last major riot in1898 in Phoebus occurred on October 18 when a riot

---

[57] "Tucker in Hampton," *Daily Press* (August 24, 1898).
[58] Ibid.
[59] Ibid.
[60] "Trouble Seems to Be Over," *Daily Press* (August 25, 1898).

ensued after a dozen rowdy soldiers from Fort Monroe tried to jump the stage while a girl was doing the "skirt dance."

Pat Egan, who owned a playhouse and saloon called the "Rialto," said that if they didn't stop then he would bring down the curtain and end the show. A soldier hurled an empty bottle at him while another soldier jumped up and started for the stage with a dozen more following him.[61]

Pat Egan reportedly shot five soldiers: killing one and seriously wounding another in the melee. Soldiers would light the theater on fire. The Phoebus Fire Department arrived to put out the flames, but the soldiers cut their hoses several times leaving the saloon to burn.[62]

T - Phoebus artist Joe Griffith captures the drama at the Rialto on October 1, 1898 (Joe Griffith).

---

[61] "Riot At Phoebus," *Daily Press* (October 19, 1898).
[62] "Virginia News," *Peninsula Enterprise* (October 22, 1898).

U - Firefighting equipment in 1898 showing the water truck (left) and hose cart (right), both pulled by horses (Tom Jackson).

Learning their lessons from August, the provost guards from Fort Monroe came to round up the soldiers and prevent them from destroying "half a dozen or more houses."[63] The dead and wounded soldiers would be transported back to Fort Monroe "while many others were arrested. The firemen remained on duty all night patrolling the town, some of them with shotguns."[64]

A grand jury of the Elizabeth City County Court, which had been investigating the riot, acquitted Egan for his role

V - Recounting the night of October 18, 1898 (Alexandria Gazette).

> following him. Egan fired a revolver at random, and then fled. A general row followed. The torch was applied to the "Rialto" and it was soon in flames. The fire hose was laid but was cut.
>
> A provost guard from Port Monroe arrived in time to prevent the destruction of a half dozen or more houses. The three wounded soldiers and the two dead ones were taken to Fort Monroe, while many others were arrested. The firemen remained on duty all night patrolling the town, some of them with shotguns.

---

[63] "Riot At Phoebus," *Daily Press* (October 19, 1898).
[64] Ibid.

in the death of the soldier John Gorman. At the same session four soldiers were charged with arson and another four were acquitted.[65] It would take more than 3 years, but Egan would receive $4,000 from the Government for the "destruction of his dwelling and other property" by United States soldiers.[66]

P.A. Fuller Tenders Resignation

On November 7, 1898, P.A. Fuller announced that he would be stepping down as Chief of the Phoebus Fire Department. According to the meeting minutes the resignation was "tendered and accepted."[67] George Henry Lancer would be nominated and elected as the 2nd Chief of the Phoebus Fire Company and P.A. Fuller would go on to build a Phoebus landmark.

One of the first decisions of the Lancer-era was standardizing the uniforms. At the meeting on January 2, 1899, it was decided that the uniform of the Phoebus Fire Department would be a "red shirt, blue pants, red belt, black necktie, black hat, red front piece except officers who were required to wear a white front piece."[68]

Yellow Fever Quarantine, 1899

The Phoebus Fire Department would also play a large role in keeping Phoebus from descending into chaos during the Yellow Fever quarantine of 1899.

It started with an outbreak at the Old Soldiers' Home on July 16 with the first deaths following on July 27. The threat of Yellow Fever was taken quite seriously at the time, especially in Hampton Roads, where a similar outbreak in Norfolk in 1855 killed upwards of 3,000. After the first deaths,

---

[65] "Special Grand Jury," *Alexandria Gazette* (November 11, 1898).
[66] "Virginia Bills," *The Times (Richmond)* (December 12, 1901).
[67] Phoebus Fire Department Meeting Minutes, (November 7, 1898).
[68] Phoebus Fire Department Meeting Minutes, (January 2, 1899).

the Home and Phoebus were quarantined. A group of hastily organized armed guards patrolled a 4-mile line between Hampton and Newport News trying to control the spread of the disease (and people). Thousands of citizens decided to take their chances and flee the area.[69]

"Fully 3,000 people have left this vicinity since the discovery of the contagion, with many of them walking out of Hampton for fear of being stopped,"[70] the *Daily Press* reported.

"The Old Point hotels have discharged their servants, there being nothing for them to do and nothing to feed them with. Businesses at Hampton, Phoebus, Old Point and Buckroe Beach have been paralyzed."[71]

Business was suspended in Phoebus and rumors spread quickly. On August 2, 1899 "Hampton closed its doors against Phoebus" only leaving Salter's Creek as an escape route. Hampton was also "entirely cut off from communication with the outside world."

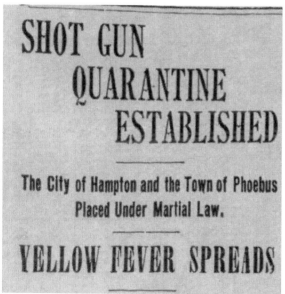

W - Headlines from August 2, 1899 (Reading Times, PA).

---

[69] "Phoebus Infected," *Daily Press* (August 2, 1899).

[70] Ibid.

[71] "Phoebus Infected," *Daily Press* (August 2, 1899).

X - The Exodus from Newport News Caused By the Yellow Fever Outbreak. Published on August 12, 1899 (Harper's Weekly).

The quarantine lasted two weeks and caused much anxiety, especially after Town Sergeant Joe Mastin contracted the disease. Mastin would later recover, but tensions were extremely high.

There were even reports of rioting outside the home of Dr. George Vanderslice on August 15. Newspapers reported that Phoebus blamed him for the outbreak, but they were found to be "absolutely groundless" later that day.[72] There was one bright spot during the quarantine. There were several reports of the Phoebus Fire Department entertaining citizens by singing and dancing throughout the ordeal. One citizen called it "their finest hour."[73]

In all, twenty soldiers at The Old Soldiers' Home died during the outbreak.

---

[72] "Phoebus All Right," *Daily Press* (August 15, 1899).

[73] Ibid.

Salty Talk

There's a funny entry in the Fire Department minutes during two months in 1896. At the meeting on August 3, 1896, there was a motion that John Kearney would be fined 25 cents for using foul language and it was quickly seconded.[74]

At the next meeting on September 7, a motion was passed that any member of the Fire Company named John Kearney would be fined at least 50 cents for each obscenity in the future. It was quickly passed as a testament to Mr. Kearney's salty tongue.[75]

Longtime fireman and current company chaplain, Don Blagg, recounted a similar story from Chief Clyde Norman decades later. Norman would sometimes deposit $5.00 in a cussing jar before a meeting saying "I'll get my money's worth" and giving a sly smile.

Phoebus Fire Department No. 1 Bell

Phoebus Fire Department No. 1 is cast on the bell which now hangs in front of the station on a pedestal of honor. The bell was forged in 1899 and hung in the belfry of the original wooden building, and subsequently on the roof in the bell tower on the current building.

The Bell now rests on a pedestal of honor in front of the Station and is used for special occasions and memorials for all fallen or deceased firefighters. The Company in Baltimore that cast the bell in 1899 is still in business and has the original record of the Order for the bell and the specifications.

---

[74] Phoebus Fire Department Meeting Minutes (August 3, 1896).
[75] Phoebus Fire Department Meeting Minutes (September 7, 1896).

Y - The fire station bell cast in 1899 (Tim Receveur).

Pride of Phoebus Spotlight
George Henry Lancer
Second and Fifth Phoebus Fire Chief
Charter Member of the Phoebus Fire
Department
Last Surviving Charter Member of the
Phoebus Fire Department
Chief of Phoebus Police
Member of the Phoebus Town Council
Life: 1865 – 1951

George Henry Lancer was both the second and the fifth captain of the Phoebus Fire Department, having served from 1898 – 1912 and again in 1918 – 1931. Together with his younger brother Frank G. Lancer, Lancer was a charter member having formed the department in 1893.

George Lancer served as a ladderman until September 7, 1896, when he was elected foreman. Mr. Lancer held that position until his election as chief of the department November 7, 1898, upon the retirement of P.A. Fuller. George remained chief until his resignation in May 1912, and then resigned due to a change in personal address. John Ferber was then elected in May 1912 as the third Fire Chief. He resigned in 1917. Frank A. Kearney was elected the fourth Fire Chief and served until his death in 1918, serving for a very short time. George Lancer had, in the meantime, moved back to Phoebus and was elected Chief in 1918 and served until 1931. He resigned a second time because he had moved to Charleston, South Carolina. Anton Alexander (Tony) Schmidt was elected as the sixth Fire Chief to replace Chief Lancer.

In addition to being fire chief for 32 years total, he was also the chief of police, and a member of the Phoebus Town Council. Lancer owned and worked at the Hotel Richelieu (also known as Lancer Brothers) and was the co-owner of Phoebus Real Estate and Insurance Company.

George Henry Lancer died on March 8, 1951, in Norfolk, Virginia, and was interred in the family lot of the Oakland Cemetery. George was the last surviving charter member of the Phoebus Fire Department.

Z - George Henry Lancer. Left: Second Phoebus Fire Chief (1898 – 1912). Right: As Fifth Phoebus Fire Chief (1918 – 1931) (Tom Jackson).

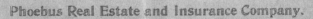

Phoebus Real Estate and Insurance Company.

I. T. JONES,   H. H. HENRY,   GEO. H. LANCER.

PROMINENT among the realty houses in this town we make special reference to the Phoebus Real Estate and Insurance Company. Mr. I. T. Jones, President, a well known member of the bar, and Messrs George Lancer, treasurer, and Hugh H. Henry, secretary, who have become known as leaders in their lines of business, which embraces a general real estate exchange that includes the buying, selling, renting and exchanging of all kinds of town and country property, negotiable loans, collecting rents managing property for non-residents, etc., as well as general Insurance agents. Their office is located on Mellen street above Mallory, until their handsome brick structure at the corner of Mellen and Mallory streets is completed.

AA - Page from "Incorporation of Phoebus", April 2, 1900 (Tom Jackson).

3 PHOEBUS DEDICATION AND REFORM: 1900-1919

At the dawning of the 20th century, there was a new optimism and push for renewal in Phoebus especially after the riots in 1898. The town held a ceremony to dedicate its new name on April 2, 1900. In the program, town leaders wrote that "for the past ten years or so, the growth of Phoebus has not kept pace with the growth of saloons, but under a strong local government this condition of things will not continue."[76] Leaders would take many steps to improve the town over the next few decades.

It was perhaps the greatest day in Phoebus history as the entire town showed up to celebrate this milestone. On its Inaugural Day, the city welcomed a host of dignitaries from across Virginia including Virginia Governor James Hoge Tyler.

BB - Phoebus Dedication – April 2, 1900 (Tony Schmidt).

The *Daily Press* wrote that "Governor Tyler was greeted by an enormous crowd at the depot on his arrival from Richmond. He was driven immediately to the [Phoebus] Sentinel office and introduced to Mayor White and the councilmen. His carriage was then driven to the head of the parade and the line moved."[77]

---

[76] Official Program for Dedication of Phoebus (April 2, 1900).
[77] "Tyler in Phoebus," *Daily Press* (April 3, 1900).

CC - Virginia Governor James Hoge Tyler at the Phoebus Sentinel building on April 2, 1900 (Tony Schmidt).

DD - Firemen in the parade during the dedication of Phoebus on April 2, 1900 (Tom Jackson).

There was a new optimism in town as well as wide calls for reform in the new century[78] as citizens tried to make the new city run as efficiently as the Fire Department. Reforms in these early days included new paved streets, sewers, sidewalks, telephone service, and additional streetcar tracks down Mellen and Mallory Streets.[79]

For the Fire Department, the city put in new fire plugs[80] and new water pipes across the city.[81] The fire plugs were painted white across the city in 1905.[82] In meeting notes from the town council in 1902, the floors and platforms in and around the engine house had become "unsafe for both the horses and apparatus" and the town council voted to approve the funds to fix them at once.[83]

EC - Firemen and horses around 1907. George Lancer is standing in front of the white horse with his hands crossed over his chest and wearing white gloves (Tom Jackson).

---

[78] "The Reform Ball Rolling," *Daily Press* (April 1, 1902).

[79] "Phoebus Sewer System," *Richmond Dispatch* (April 25, 1902).

[80] "Needed Improvements Planned for Phoebus," *Daily Press* (June 8, 1906).

[81] Town Council Meeting Notes (February 20, 1902).

[82] "Will Have Fountain," *Daily Press* (July 21, 1905).

[83] Town Council Meeting Notes (February 20, 1902).

Fairs and Parades

As the new century kicked off, members of the Fire Department became even more engaged with the community, especially since the volunteers needed funds from the public to purchase equipment. Starting in 1900, the Fire Department started putting flowers on the graves of dead firemen every Memorial Day. The Phoebus community would donate flowers to the fire department each year.[84]

The Fire Department created the yearly Firemen's Fair to raise funds and one of the largest early fairs was held in 1905. It was originally scheduled to last four days but became so popular that it ran for an additional two days. The purpose of the fair was to raise funds to buy gum suits for the men.[85]

The fair included a parade with several floats, military companies, and fire departments from neighboring Hampton and Newport News.

FF - Mellen Street with new sidewalks in 1900 (LVA photo).

---

[84] "Firemen, Legion to Place Flowers on Graves Today," *Daily Press* (May 30, 1938).
[85] "Now in Full Blast," *Daily Press* (May 11, 1905).

After the first night on May 9, 1905, the *Daily Press* reported "the Phoebus firemen's fair launched last night under the most auspicious circumstances. In fact, if the opening night is an omen the firemen will certainly make good their claims that this is to be the banner entertainment gotten up by the department."[86]

"Almost from the time that the big doors to the engine house were swung open until midnight a crowd thronged the building and several booths did a thriving business. The opening of the parade was signaled by one of the largest and most imposing parades that Phoebus has ever seen. The fair will run for four nights and each evening promises a new and novel program of entertainment. Tonight it is expected that the crowd will be even larger than that in attendance last evening."[87]

The 1905 Firemen's Fair was a smashing success[88] and finally ended on May 16 with a dance in honor of the "ladies who have made the fair one of the most successful ever."[89]

This is how the *Phoebus Sentinel* described the fair on May 20, 1905:

"The firemen's fair closed last Tuesday night and it was one of the most successful events of the kind ever held in Phoebus, all things considered. The fair was held six days and during that time a liberal sum was realized. Mr. Frank A. Kearney, chairman of the committee, says he cannot state just now the exact amount that was realized, as a number of contributions are still out, but he is positive the amount will exceed $1,000. Thursday night a most delightful dance was tendered the ladies who assisted at the fair and a most enjoyable evening was spent. There were fully 200 people present and during the evening, ice cream and cake were served."[90]

The fairs would be an important part of Phoebus life and each one would be used to raise funds to help the Phoebus Fire Department purchase needed equipment. In 1923, the goal was to raise funds for a "motorized hook and ladder truck"[91] and the Fire Department needed funds in 1927 in

---

[86] "Now in Full Blast," *Daily Press* (May 11, 1905).

[87] Ibid.

[88] "To Be Continued," *Daily Press* (May 14, 1905).

[89] "Closes Tonight," *Daily Press* (May 16, 1905).

[90] "A Great Success," *Phoebus Sentinel* (May 20, 1905).

[91] "Firemen's Fair in Phoebus is Opened," *Daily Press* (May 1, 1923).

order to pay off the "indebtedness for the new pumper".[92]

GG - Men working on an early 500-gallon water pumper (Tom Jackson).

HH - Parade during the Firemen's Fair down Mellen Street near The American Theatre

---

[92] "Phoebus Ladies Meet Thursday," *Daily Press* (Mach 23, 1927).

around 1915 (Tom Jackson).

Conventions and Camaraderie

In 1886, the Virginia State Firemen's Association (now the Virginia State Firefighter's Association) was formed and the organization started hosting yearly conventions across the state in a different city each year.

The Phoebus Fire Department began participating regularly in the conventions in the early 1900s. The convention would promote skills competitions between the departments using ladders and hoses as well as elaborate parades in each city.

Competitions included events like "1 Man Hose," "4 Man Hose," "4 Man Ladder (14 foot)," "4 Man Ladder (20 foot)," "6 Man Ladder," and many more. The conventions would also be a time to share best practices across the state at a time when the capabilities of fire departments were changing rapidly.[93]

Phoebus would host the convention in 1930 and again in 1953 (after consolidation with Hampton). When traveling, it wasn't unusual for the Phoebus fire department to bring upwards of eighty[94] or ninety[95] men to the conventions despite being a small city.

Phoebus also made trips around the country to build ties with other communities including those in Pennsylvania and New York. In one community in Mount Carmel, Pennsylvania, the local newspapers expressed their excitement that the Phoebus Fire Department was visiting in October 1908.[96]

"They struck the town at 7 o'clock last night, on the Pennsylvania train, and one minute after they were in our midst they owned Mount Carmel. And they got our old burg without a struggle. It was just simply handed to them. Firemen, band and escort, they number seventy-six men perfect specimens of American manhood. We are proud to have them as our guests. They came North to attend the Pennsylvania State Firemen's convention at Shamokin and are making Mount Carmel their headquarters during the

---

[93] "Details are Arranged for Firemen's Parade," *Daily Press* (August 28, 1930).
[94] "Delegates Leave Tonight," *Daily Press* (August 23, 1910).
[95] "Phoebus Great Showing," *Daily Press* (August 27, 1909).
[96] "Our Guests, The Virginia Firemen," *Mount Carmel Item* (October 7, 1908).

sessions, having accepted an invitation extended by the Anthracite Fire Company several months ago."

"The Virginians were met at the station by the Anthracite, American and Clover fire companies, with the Anthracite Band. Three rousing cheers were given them as they alighted from the train, and then a parade was formed. Along the line of march thousands of our people were congregated, and they were greeted with volumes of cheers, fireworks, and enthusiasm. The populace broke loose, and it was no effort for the Phoebus men to know and feel that they were welcome here."[97]

The article also made a point that Phoebus had brought three Jewish members in its delegation: Morris Cooper, F.J. Carmel, and I.A.. Saunders.[98]

II - Phoebus Fire Department hat in the early part of the 20th century.

The Mount Carmel article also took a keen liking to future Chief Frank A. Kearney. "Foreman Kearney's manly form is the envy of the company. He had no less than six waitresses attending to his wants this morning. And Frank's married at that."[99]

Phoebus was also a destination for many fire companies thanks to its numerous hotels and saloons. The Phoebus Fire Department also built

---

[97] "Our Guests, The Virginia Firemen," *Mount Carmel Item* (October 7, 1908).
[98] Ibid.
[99] Ibid.

long-lasting bonds with many fire departments around the country. One of the more prominent bonds was with the Rex Hook and Ladder Company Number 1 from York, Pennsylvania. The two cities exchanged visits each year, with Phoebus visiting York one year and York visiting Phoebus the next, and so on.[100] York visited Phoebus on October 19-20, 1910 and lots of pomp and circumstance accompanied their two days in Phoebus.

Here's some of the coverage from the *Daily Press* that year: "After capturing Phoebus early yesterday morning, the members of the Rex Hook and Ladder Company No. 1. of York, were last night the guests of honor at a banquet in the Bank of Phoebus building, tendered them by the Phoebus firemen. The banquet hall was handsomely decorated for the occasion and there were ten big tables, covered with tempting viands."[101]

"After the banqueters had done full justice to the menu, Foreman Frank A. Kearney, of the Phoebus department, who is always at home as a toastmaster, rapped for order."[102]

"Mr. Kearney in a few well-chosen words presented [Phoebus] Mayor L.P. Furness, who gave the visitors a hearty welcome to the city, and expressed the hope that their stay here would prove one of enjoyment, as he felt certain their presence was a source of great pleasure to the Phoebus firemen and the people generally of the town."[103]

"Mayor William Weaver, of York, a very pleasing speaker, responded to the welcoming address and brought down the house several times with his witticisms on the members of his company. Mayor Weaver said that he voiced the sentiment of his firemen in saying that all were glad to be in Phoebus. It is though the 'heavens had opened up to them.'"[104]

The guests from York had two full days of activities while in the area. The York firemen arrived at Old Point on the steamer Columbia from Baltimore at 5:30am on Wednesday, October 19 and were met on the wharf by the entire membership of the Phoebus fire company.

"The visitors were brought to Mill Creek bridge on special cars and then

---

[100] "Phoebus Fire Co. Trophies Unusual," *Daily Press* (December 8, 1964).
[101] "York Firemen Take the Town of Phoebus," *Daily Press* (October 20, 1910).
[102] Ibid.
[103] Ibid.
[104] Ibid.

marched to the engine house, where light refreshments were served. They were then taken to the Palm, Washington and Palace hotels, where they were quartered during their visit to Phoebus."

"At 9 o'clock the Pennsylvanians were taken to the National Soldiers' Home, where they inspected the big institution for the disabled veterans of Uncle Sam's Army and Navy."[105]

Here is their dinner menu from the banquet held in the Bank of Phoebus on the opening night of their visit on October 19, 1910:

The banquet hall was handsomely decorated for the occasion and there were ten big tables, covered with tempting viands.

The menu.

OYSTERS

Lynnhaven Raw   Pickled la Haas
Fried a la Davis

CRABS

Devilede a la Johnson

MEATS

Smithfield Ham   Ham au-conti
Sliced Ox Tongue—York Style
Capon a la surprise

Chicken Salad   Cold Slaw
Deviled Eggs   Swiss Cheese
Sliced Tomatoes   Celery   Pickles
Assorted Fruits   Cake
Bottled Refreshments—Phoebus Style

After the banqueters had done full justice to the menu, Foreman Frank A. Kearney, of the Phoebus department, who is always at home as a toastmaster, rapped for order.

JJ - Dinner menu for October 19, 1910 in Phoebus for the York, Pennsylvania firemen (Daily Press).

---

[105] "York Firemen Take the Town of Phoebus," *Daily Press* (October 20, 1910).

KK – Phoebus Fire Department Badge from around 1930 (Tom Jackson).

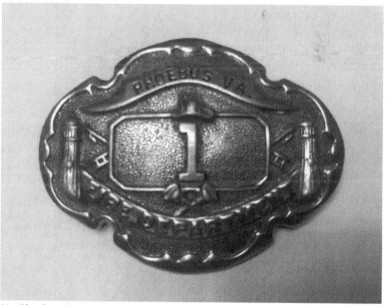

LL - Phoebus Fire Department belt buckle from between 1920-1940 (Tom Jackson).

MM - Phoebus Fire Department No.1 around 1910. Fire Chief George Lancer is pictured in the suit in the front row (Tom Jackson).

NN - Group photo around 1910 (Tony Schmidt).

OO - P.A. Fuller's Fire Department building in 1915 (Hampton Public Library).

PP - Medals presented to members of the York, Pennsylvania and Niagara Falls Fire Departments on their visit to Phoebus in September 1913 (Tom Jackson).

QQ - Ribbons given out to celebrate the visit of the York, Pennsylvania firemen to Phoebus on October 19-20, 1910 (Tony Schmidt).

Fire Department and City Hall headquarters on Hope Street around 1905 (Tony Schmidt photo).

Solid Coal Trumpet

A *Daily Press* article from 1964 mentions many of the awards on display at the Phoebus Fire Company.

"The old Phoebus Fire Department for many years visited numerous other cities in the East to participate in civic and fire department parades. Many of the trophies now on display in the firehouse were won by marching company in out-of-town and out-of-state parades." These include an "unusual "solid coal trumpet."[106]

The trumpet was carved from a "solid piece of coal nearly two feet tall and five inches around at its base. The coal has been highly polished so that it resembles onyx and it does not transfer a black stain when it is rubbed." The trumpet was presented to Phoebus by the fire department at Shamokin, Pennsylvania on September 2, 1913.[107]

---

[106] "Phoebus Fire Co. Trophies Unusual," *Daily Press* (December 8, 1964).
[107] Ibid.

PHOEBUS FIRE COMPANY TROPHIES

Solid coal trumpet, left, won at Shamokin, Pa., in 1913, has place of honor among Phoebus Fire Company trophies won over the years since 1893. Other honored trophies of the company include, starting second from left, a silver trumpet from York, Pa., 1908; silver trumpet from Reading, Pa., 1914; and silver cup from Norristown, Pa., exact date unknown. With the trophies is Gilbert W. Johnson, chief of the Phoebus Fire Company.

RR - Fireman Gilbert W. Johnson with the Fire Company's solid coal trumpet in 1964 (Daily Press).

55 - Ornamental anthracite speaking trumpet presented to the Phoebus Fire Company in 1913 (Courtesy of the Hampton History Museum – ID # L2017.9.1).

Out of Control Hose Wagon

Firefighting has always been a dangerous business, but it was even more so in the early days without today's protective gear and using horses instead of trucks.

FIREMAN DAVIS HURT

Thrown From Hose Cart While Responding to Alarm.

HE WAS SERIOUSLY INJURED

Bit Broke and Horse Ran Away With Hose Wagon, Striking Telegraph Pole and Plunging Through Fence— Pole of Hose Wagon Broken.

TT - Report of hose wagon accident on May 10, 1905 (Daily Press).

This is brought to life by an accident that occurred in May 1905 when responding to a explosion of a gas stove at the home of George Lancer. According to the report, the hose wagon was in a major accident on May 9 when driver Thomas M. Jones reported that the bridle broke and the horse became unmanageable as the wagon turned onto Chesapeake Avenue which is near the west end of Mellen Street. The horse and wagon ran into a telegraph pole and went through a wooden fence where Jones was thrown from the cart and injured.

The worst injuring occurred to fireman R.L. Davis who was riding in the cart and was tossed violently to the ground and knocked unconscious. Dr. George K. Vanderslice examined Davis and expected him to make a recovery.[108]

New Tractor Arrives

In October 1916, Phoebus spent a whopping $4,200 on a "splendid, new" motor tractor for the fire company. "The tractor is one of the most complete machines and the motorizing of the Phoebus Fire Department is looked on as a big thing to that town."

---

[108] "Fireman Davis Hurt," *Daily Press* (May 10, 1905).

"Arrangements for the big parade in honor of the arrival of the tractor and the changing of the department from horses to tractor next Tuesday are going ahead nicely."[109]

NEW MOTOR TRACTOR FOR PHOEBUS ARRIVES

The splendid new $4,200 motor tractor for the Phoebus fire department arrived in Norfolk yesterday, and will be brought to Phoebus for delivery to the department today. The tractor is one of the most complete machines and the motorizing of the Phoebus department is looked upon as a big thing to that town.

Arrangements for the big parade in honor of the arrival of the tractor and the changing of the department from horses to tractor next Tuesday are going ahead nicely. The committee yesterday received word that the department of Newport News will also attend, as will the departments from Riverview and George Wythe.

The Newport News shipyard band will march at the head of the Phoebus department in the parade.

UU - Article on new fire truck on October 16, 1916 (Daily Press).

[109] "New Motor Tractor for Phoebus Arrives," *Daily Press* (October 16, 1916).

Gone But Never Forgotten

The Phoebus Fire Company has always had a mix of strong personalities and this even applied to their horses. As the 20th century started and the town moved away from horse-drawn apparatus and towards mechanized fire trucks, the question came up about what to do with the obsolete horses.

At the November 7, 1916 the Town Council decided the fate of the four horses. "The question of the disposition of the Fire Department horses was discussed at length after which J.W. Craigs moved that the Recorder advertise the two old horses for sale and sell them to the highest bidder for cash as soon as practicable, and that the two younger and best horses be retrained for the use of the Street Department. The motion was unanimously carried."[110]

VV – The legendary Phoebus horses (Tom Jackson).

The Street Department was the equivalent of the modern day trash pick-up so the two remaining horses were to be trained to travel around Phoebus and pick-up garbage all day, which was a sad fate for animals who were accustomed to a much more exciting lifestyle.

At the next Town Council meeting on December 5, 1916, things do not

---

[110] Town Council Meeting Notes, (November 7, 1916).

appear to be going well in the retraining process. J.W. Craigs suggests that it might be a good idea to get a "motor vehicle for the street work and do away with horses to cut down on expenses."[111]

There are reports that in late December 1916 that a somewhat serious (and somewhat hilarious) incident occurred with one of the horses picking up trash for the Street Department. The Phoebus Fire Company had a system of bells that corresponded to each of the five wards where the fire was taking place and extra bells if the fire was taking place further away like Hampton or Fort Monroe.

It turns out that one of the horses knew the location of the bells as well. He was hauling a huge bucket of waste when a series of bells rang out in 1916. The horse decided to help his friends at the fire company and it took off and ran across town dragging trash along the way. You can imagine the look of surprise on the firemen's faces when their noble steed showed up at the fire.

Sadly, Mayor Dixon didn't appreciate the animal's heart. At the January 2, 1917 Town Council meeting, "the Mayor reported that one of the horses belonging to the town and used in the Street Department was a runaway and that he thought it dangerous for the town to own such an animal.

Whereupon J.W. Craig moved that the Mayor, R.J. Copeland, and C.A. Eacho be appointed to a committee to dispose of the horse to the best advantage and use their own judgement in replacing him with mules or horses as they deem best. The motion was unanimously carried."[112]

The final mention of the horses comes on February 6, 1917. "The Special Committee on disposal of the horses, appointed at the last meeting of the Council, reported by C.A. Eacho that both of the horses of the Street Department were gone. With one set of double harness, traded or exchanged for two good mules, and that the two mules are giving excellent service."[113]

Phoebus Saved By an Exploding Whiskey Barrel?

In September 1905, the Phoebus firemen held a drill one Thursday evening which was witnessed by many townspeople and some visitors. An alarm

---

[111] Town Council Meeting Notes, (December 5, 1916).
[112] Town Council Meeting Notes, (January 2, 1917).
[113] Town Council Meeting Notes, (February 6, 1917).

was sounded from the 3rd ward and about 45 members responded. The engine and wagon then went to the corner of Mallory and Mellen Street and a very efficient drill took place there. "After the drill the boys were tendered a reception by the citizens committee. Chief George H. Lancer and Foreman F.A. Kearney thanked the committee and citizens of our town for their kindness toward the department. Mr. E. M. Tennis and W.F. Clark responded. They both praised the work of the department. The department gave a vote of thanks to the citizens committee and the Big Four Quartette rendered several selections under the leadership of Prof. W. Fountain."[114]

In about 2 months, the Phoebus Fire Department would be greatly tested in the same exact location.

One of the biggest fires in Phoebus history took place on Saturday morning, November 4, 1905 and reports seem to indicate that if not for an exploding whiskey barrel then the Phoebus business district may have been burned to the ground.

The *Daily Press* reported on a "big blaze" that reportedly started in the Edney & Rawles' Saloon on the corner of Mellen and Mallory Streets. Mr. Edney disputed that report and he claimed that the blaze started next door at Quong Wah Laundry at 5 East Mellen Street. Regardless of where it started, the fire would keep going and jump to the next building owned by J. Levensky.[115]

"When the blaze was discovered it had gained considerable headway, although the lack of water greatly handicapped the fire department and is possibly the cause of the entire destruction of the buildings. As soon as the fire was reported to the engine house Assistant Town Treasurer Phillips, Mr. A.M. Hanger and Policeman Harry Simkins hitched the horses to the fire-fighting apparatus. Driver Thomas Jones was absent from the engine house at the time and Mr. E. O. Hunt mounted the hose wagon and speeded his horses to the scene of the blaze."[116]

"When the firemen and apparatus reached the corner of the two streets they found that the water pressure was insufficient and a telephone message was hurriedly gotten through to the headquarters of the water company at Lee Hall, requesting that the water be turned on immediately. It took about twenty minutes to accomplish this and by this time the entire two-story

---

[114] "Firemen Drill in Public," *Phoebus Sentinel* (September 2, 1905).
[115] "Phoebus Town Has Big Blaze," *Daily Press* (November 5, 1905).
[116] Ibid.

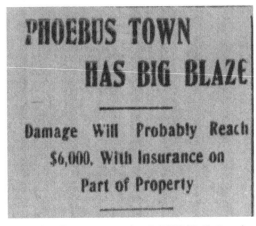

PHOEBUS TOWN HAS BIG BLAZE

Damage Will Probably Reach $6,000, With Insurance on Part of Property

WW - Headline on November 5, 1905 (Daily Press).

building known as Edney & Rawles' saloon was enveloped in flames. The fire soon jumped over to the Chinese laundry and later leaped to the building occupied by J. Levensky as a shoemaking and repair shop. Fearing that the flames would get beyond control of the Phoebus firemen and that the entire section along Mellen street, which consists of frame buildings, would be consumed, the Hampton Normal School and Fort Monroe fire departments were requested to come to Phoebus at once."[117]

"All of the firefighting companies responded promptly and. although a short delay held the Hampton department on the Soldiers' Home bridge, the local firemen reached the scene in time to render their Phoebus brothers much assistance. The Normal School department was also quick in responding and like the firemen of Hampton went to work earnest to check the flames. The department from Fort Monroe was prompt, but as three companies were at work and it was evident that the flames could be controlled. Mayor Louis P. Furness thanked the Fort Monroe fighters and told them that unless a fresh outbreak occurred their service would not be necessary.[118]

"After combating the flames for about an hour the fire was under control, doing damages as stated to three buildings and several outbuildings at the rear of the saloon. The building occupied by Messrs. Edney & Rawles was totally destroyed. It was owned by Messrs Frank A. and William Kearney and was valued at $3,000. The two-story frame structure occupied by J. Levensky was the property of Washington Diggs, colored, and was probably worth $750 Washington Diggs also owned. the building in which the laundry was conducted. This structure was estimated to be worth about $250. The Kearney Brothers carried $1,500. insurance on their buildings and it If said that Washington Diggs was also partly insured. The entire stock of liquors and furniture of Messrs. Edney & Rawles was consumed.

---

[117] "Phoebus Town Has Big Blaze," *Daily Press* (November 5, 1905).
[118] "Phoebus Town Has Big Blaze," *Daily Press* (November 5, 1905).

Mr. Edney stated that he had, more than $2,500 worth of stock in his saloon and that, he carried $1,000 insurance on the stock. Mr. Levensky's loss is a severe one as he had not a cent's worth of insurance, either on his tools, stock of leather, or household furniture. Mr. Levensky's family lived over the shop."[119]

"During the progress of the blaze Firemen [Hugh C.] Briggeman, [R] Phillips and [John] Byrne were forced to jump from the roof of the corner building on account of wires. Mr. Byrne was painfully shaken up, although an examination by Dr. George K. Vanderslice developed the fact that no bones were broken. Mr. Phillips also suffered from a burn on the face. When the fire was discovered a telephone message was sent to the office of the Newport News and Old Point Railway and Electric Company asking that the current, be cut off, as there is a network of wires just at the corner where the blaze started. The request was complied with and this action no doubt, saved other firemen from injuries by coming in contact with the live wires. The entire lower end of the railway was temporarily tied up by the cutting off of the current."[120]

"Several hundred persons from Hampton went to Phoebus to see the fire. Naturally nearly the entire population of Phoebus was out to watch the battle of the firemen with the flames. During the fire the saloon of Messrs. Lancer Brothers, on the opposite side of the street, caught fire and was considerably damaged, especially in breaking window glasses. Glasses in the stores of Cooper Brothers, Charles Matar and W. H. Hopkins were broken by the heat, from the fire in the buildings on the opposite side of the street."

In an article a week later, the Phoebus Sentinel would claim that an exploding barrel of whiskey saved the Phoebus business district from utter destruction.

"Thousands of people saw the big fire at the corner of Mellen and Mallory streets last Saturday morning, but few are aware of the fact that the explosion of a barrel of whiskey saved the business portion of Phoebus from being burned, such is the case, however, and the merchants now doing business along Mellen street between Mallory and Hope streets, may thank a kind Providence for exploding the barrel at such an opportune time."[121]

---

[119] "Phoebus Town Has Big Blaze," *Daily Press* (November 5, 1905).
[120] Ibid.
[121] "Phoebus' Big Blaze," Phoebus Sentinel (November 11, 1905).

FIRE THREATENS PHOEBUS.

Barrel of Whisky Explodes and Firemen Narrowly Escape.

Special to The Washington Post.

Newport News, Va., Nov. 4.—Fire in the business center of Phoebus to-day threatened to destroy the town, but was brought under control after it had burned the cook shop of Alexander Smith and had gutted Edney's saloon and Leneskey's shoe shop. The total loss will amount to $17,000, largely covered by insurance. The fire is believed to have originated from a gasoline stove in the cook shop. While the saloon was burning, a barrel of whisky exploded and blew down the side wall of the building. There were a number of narrow escapes from death on the part of the firemen fighting the blaze.

XX - *Washington Post headline on November 5, 1905.*

"Just when the fire was at its worst and when the fruit and confectionary store of Malar Brothers just across the street took fire, a barrel of whiskey in the burning building exploded, causing the whole front of the burning building to topple over, thus reducing the intense heat on the opposite side of the street. All heard the report and saw the wall of flames fall in, but few knew what caused it."[122]

"After the fire Mr. Frank A. Kearney stated that he would sue the water company for damages, alleging that the low pressure of water at the time of the fire was responsible for his loss. It was also given out that the Kearney Brothers would immediately rebuild after their losses have been adjusted by the insurance people."[123]

Serial Arsonist in Phoebus?

Phoebus witnessed a large string of arsons between 1900-1905. Robert E. Wilson, better known as R.E. Wilson, ran a coal, oil, and wood store on Mallory Street and saw at least five arson attempts in 1900 and 1901 alone. Heinickel's Bakery at 20 East Mellen Street saw two arson attempts in 1901 using coal oil to start the fire, a common element in the arsons.

---

[122] "Phoebus' Big Blaze," Phoebus Sentinel (November 11, 1905).
[123] "Phoebus Town Has Big Blaze," *Daily Press* (November 5, 1905).

YY - R.E. Wilson Coal and Oil on Mallory Street in 1915 (Hampton Public Library).

ZZ - Heinickel's Bakery opened in 1895 on 20 East Mellen Street (Hampton Public Library).

Barnes Corner would see another fire as well, this one started by arson in 1904. An early morning fire on January 20, 1904 destroyed two buildings, one building was occupied by B. A. Lively, as a grocery, and the other building was occupied by Virginia Thompson and three other women. The fire was ruled as arson. "The buildings burned so rapidly that they are supposed to have been fired all around. Lively stated that he found an oil can near the building this morning."[124]

Another outbreak in 1905 prompted the Daily Press to label the arsonist the "Fire Fiend".[125] "For several days the people of Phoebus have been much wrought up over the presence of a supposed 'fire fiend,' and the officers of the town have been at work endeavoring to unravel the mysterious blazes. It was thought that in as much as the two buildings destroyed were unoccupied that probably the fires were started in a spirit of 'fun,' but the police authorities cannot see a joke in so serious a matter. The crime of arson in Virginia is punishable by either death or a long term in the Virginia penitentiary."[126]

HELD UPON SUSPICION.

Two Men at Phoebus Were Charged with Incendiarism.

Special to The Washington Post.

Newport News, Va., Dec. 20.—In the Phoebus Police Court to-day Walter Fontaine and Edward T. Morton were placed under $5,000 bail as suspicious characters. The men were up on the charge of setting fire to two houses in Phoebus, but the evidence was not sufficient for a conviction.

The people of the town have been much aroused by several recent fires, and there has been talk of lynching if the firebugs are caught. A policeman testified that Morton and Fontaine were seen running from one of the houses set on fire shortly before the blaze was discovered.

AAA - Washington Post headline on December 21, 1905.

Three men were arrested on December 19, 1905 as prime suspects in the arson, including a bartender at the Roseland Club Hotel, but they were all released due to lack of evidence two days later.[127] These were just a few of the arsons that we discovered in the early days of the century and we could find no convictions for arson in newspaper records.

Regardless of the cause of the fire, the Phoebus Fire Department always stood ready to answer the call. A massive fire in December 1909 started in a shed to the rear of Charles Humphrey's barbershop on Mellen Street. G. G. Congdon had a drug store next door [108 East Mellen Street] and he came out and saw the flames.

---

[124] "Fire in Phoebus," *Daily Press* (January 21, 1904).

[125] "Fire Fiend Scared the Town," *Daily Press* (December 19, 1905).

[126] Ibid.

[127] "Alleged 'Fire Bugs' Get Scotch Verdict," *Daily Press* (December 21, 1905).

"At this time two flames were leaping above the little structure and it looked as though the entire block of frame buildings, from Hope to Curry Streets, along Mellen Street would be destroyed."[128] Mr. Congdon hurriedly gave the alarm and the Phoebus Fire Department was on the scene in a few minutes. The firemen soon got two streams of water playing on the flames, while additional streams were put on the Congdon drug store and Tony Nicoletta's music store." Mr. Nicoletta later reported damage of $200 as a "handsome piano and a great deal of sheet music were drenched by the water."[129]

BUSINESS BLOCK IN PHOEBUS THREATENED

Blaze in Shed Seemed Likely to Spread from Structure on Mellen Street.

Considerable uneasiness was caused among the business men in Phoebus last night by a fire, which was found burning in the shed just in the rear of Charles Humphreys' barber shop, in Mellen street, shortly before 9 o'clock. The blaze was discovered by Mr. G. G. Congdon, whose drug store is just one door to the south of the barber shop. At this time two flames were leaping over the little structure and it looked as though the entire block of frame buildings, from Hope to Curry streets, along Mellen street, would be destroyed.

BBB - Headline from December 17, 1909 (Daily Press).

A fire of unimaginable scale would be in store for the Phoebus Fire Department, and all of Hampton Roads, just a few years later.

---

[128] "Business Block in Phoebus Threatened," *Daily Press* (December 17, 1909).
[129] Ibid.

CCC - Panoramic photo of Phoebus Fire Department around 1918 with zoom images below- Gift of K. Sylvia Snow (Courtesy of the Hampton History Museum - ID: 2005.12.1)

DDD –Left to right: Ishmael Bushrod Giddings, Lewis Handle, and an unidentified fireman in 1909 (Michele Handle McPherson).

Pride of Phoebus Spotlight
Frank A. Kearney
Phoebus Fire Chief
Member of the First Phoebus Town Council
Life: 1878 – 1918

Frank A. Kearney was a leading citizen of Phoebus and was the active Fire Chief when he died during the Spanish Flu epidemic on October 23, 1918. Kearney was a member of the first Phoebus Town Council when the town consolidated in 1900 and served for several terms.

Kearney was the general manager of the Hampton Roads Engineering and Construction Company. Kearney invested his money in real estate and became one of the largest property owners in town. Kearney lived on Curry Street and he worked with his brother William J. Kearney at their saloon called The Philadelphia Club on the corner of Mellen and Curry Streets.

In his obituary in the *Daily Press* on October 24, 1918, it was written that he was "one of the most beloved citizens of Phoebus" and "probably no death in this community in years will bring more genuine sorrow to the homes of the town of Phoebus than the taking away of Frank Kearney."[130]

"News of the death of Mr. Kearney spread over Hampton and Phoebus quickly and from all sides the news came as a shock and a feeling that the lower peninsula had lost one of its most useful citizens, while Phoebus has sustained a loss which will be unfilled for many years."[131]

---

[130] "Frank A. Kearney Dies in Phoebus from Influenza," *Daily Press* (October 24, 1918).
[131] Ibid.

ATTENTION PHOEBUS FIREMEN

All members of the Phoebus Fire Department will assemble at the engine house at 1 o'clock this (Friday) afternoon for the purpose of attending the funeral of our honored late chief, Frank A. Kearney.

Wear full uniform, white gloves and badges.

By order of the acting chief.

EDWARD C. KAISER,
· Secretary.

In the Phoebus Fire Department hangs a document called *Resolutions of Respect* that was adopted on November 3, 1918. It reads:

"Resolved, That in the death of Frank A. Kearney, the Department has lost a brother who was always active and zealous in his work as a Fireman, ever ready to risk his life in the discharge of his duties, prompt to advance the interests of the Department, devoted to its welfare and prosperity; one who was wise in counsel and fearless in action, an honest and upright man, who virtues endeared him not only to his brethren of this Department, but to all of his fellow citizens."

EEE - UU - Headline from October 24, 1918 (Daily Press).

FRANK A. KEARNEY,
Councilman Second Ward,

FFF - Frank A. Kearney as a 22-year-old Town Councilman in 1900.

4 THE CHAMBERLIN HOTEL FIRE: 1920

At the end of the 19th Century, one of the greatest hotels in American history started to take shape at Old Point Comfort. The Hygeia Hotel was already a tourist destination when the Chamberlin Hotel opened next door in 1896. The Chamberlin Hotel was constructed as a wooden structure covered with bricks in the Queen Anne style. The 450 room hotel was designed by architect Paul J. Pelz, who also designed the Library of Congress,[132] and the hotel was built by the Holtzclaw Brothers.[133] The wooden infrastructure would spell its doom less than a quarter century later.

Since it was located on a military post, the hotel required special permission from Congress.[134] Founder John Chamberlin was a famed restaurant owner in Washington, DC. It would be through food that Chamberlin would befriend President Grover Cleveland and this connection would secure the permits to build the hotel.

In newspaper accounts of the era, Chamberlin's Maryland Street restaurant and club catered to the upper crust of society in Washington, DC.[135] Chamberlin was legendary for his extremely high prices. "Chamberlin prided himself on the altitude of his rates, as well as the excellence of his cuisine."[136] There's a humorous account of Colonel Dick Wintersmith of Kentucky, a well-known character around Washington, DC, who wanted beef and onions for dinner. The trouble was that the Colonel was heading to the theater with a group of ladies afterwards and didn't want to smell like onions. "Don't worry Uncle Dick," said his nephew at the table, "when Chamberlin brings you the bill it will definitely take your breath away."[137]

In his early days as President, Grover Cleveland called upon Chamberlin for

---

[132] "Famous Resort," *Daily Press* (March 8, 1920).

[133] "Hotel Chamberlin Destroyed By Flames," *Daily Press* (March 8, 1920).

[134] "Historic Romance of the Chamberlin," *Daily Press* (March 9, 1920).

[135] Mark St. John Erickson, "Hotel Chamberlin boosted Hampton resort's status" (Daily Press, March 8, 2018).

[136] "Stories of John Chamberlin," *The Liberty Vindicator (Liberty, Texas)* (July 23, 1897).

[137] Ibid.

help in the White House kitchen. He was looking for someone who could cook oysters, clams, crabs, and terrapin in the Maryland style. Chamberlin sent him a cook for the summer when business was slow and an instant friendship developed.[138]

With Chamberlin's connections, the permits were acquired and construction on the first Chamberlin Hotel began in 1887. It took nine years to complete. Here's an account from the Norfolk Virginian on its opening on Friday, April 5, 1896:

GGG - The First Chamberlin in 1905. The sign on the wharf indicates trolley service to Phoebus and the Hampton Institute (Library of Congress Prints and Photographs Division).

"One of the largest, and the handsomest hotel in America was formally opened for the patronage of the public yesterday, when the Chamberlin Hotel at Old Point threw open its doors. It is seldom that so many people of prominence are gathered together as were under the roof of the new hostelry last night, for there were Cabinet officials, army officials of high rank, Senators, Congressmen, Governors of states, and society people present.

The first guest registered at the new hotel was Mr. W. H. Kimberly, of Baltimore, who placed his name on the register Friday evening. He was soon followed by John Eraser, wife, and daughter, who were assigned to room 478. This was the first room assigned to a guest. Yesterday every incoming- train and boat brought crowds, and at 7 o'clock the big register was closed, every room having been filled. Some 500 people were installed in the handsome rooms. The Washington steamer in the morning brought

---

[138] Adrian Miller, *The President's Kitchen Cabinet: The Story of the African Americans Who Have Fed Our First Families, from the Washingtons to the Obamas* (Chapel Hill, NC: University of North Carolina Press, 2017), 98.

down Hon. H. A. Herbert. Secretary of the Navy; General Nelson A. Miles, of the Army; ex-Senator Butler, Senator Vest of Missouri; Senator Blackburn, of Kentucky; and a score of others, especially invited to attend the opening. As each succeeding boat arrived half a hundred guests placed their names on the register."[139]

"There are 400 sleeping rooms, with accommodations for 600 guests. The sleeping rooms are fitted up with the most expensive furniture. In oak, brass, walnut, maple, and mahogany. The darker woods, such as walnut and mahogany, are inlaid with tasteful design in maple and pearl. The carpets are of the finest and of a large variety of patterns. These sleeping rooms are located on all six of floors and are thoroughly ventilated."[140]

The Chamberlin Hotel would serve as a center of tourism for the Peninsula throughout the next 24 years, most notably during the Jamestown Exposition of 1907. A catastrophic fire would start in the late afternoon of March 7, 1920 and by the morning the future of the region would be forever changed.

HHH - Sailors coming ashore in 1896. The original Chamberlin Hotel is located on the left while the second Hygeia Hotel sits to the right (Library of Congress).

---

[139] "In a Blaze of Glory," *The Norfolk Virginian* (April 5, 1896).
[140] Ibid.

"Today, you don't see the wharf. You don't see the beach. You only see the last surviving hotel [the second Chamberlin Hotel]. So people don't realize the scale of what was here," says John V. Quarstein, co-author of the 2009 book "Old Point Comfort Resort: Hospitality, Health and History on Virginia's Chesapeake Bay."[141]

III - Fire rages out of control on the afternoon of March 7, 1920 (Daily Press).

The first flames started around 4:45pm on March 7, 1920 and many of the 400-hotel guest were preparing for dinner.[142] Manager George F. Adams had just returned to the hotel after an afternoon of golf in Phoebus. The fire alarms were immediately sounded to the Chamberlin fire fighting force and to Fort Monroe.

This was immediately followed by a general alarm to Phoebus, Hampton, the Old Soldiers' Home, Newport News, Camp Eustis, and Langley Field and within half an hour there were "several thousand on the scene, and fire apparatus from all surrounding points were placing streams of water on the blaze."[143]

The entire Phoebus Fire Department would arrive to battle the blaze, but

---

[141] Mark St. John Erickson, "Hotel Chamberlin boosted Hampton resort's status" (Daily Press, March 8, 2018).
[142] Mark St. John Erickson, "Landmark Chamberlin Hotel burns in March 1920 fire" (Daily Press, March 13, 2014).
[143] "Hotel Chamberlin Destroyed By Flames," *Daily Press* (March 8, 1920).

the firefighting equipment of the day was woefully inadequate to battle a large fire in the massive five-story wooden hotel.

And this was no ordinary fire and it also began at the worst possible spot. "The blaze started almost in the very center of the building. This made it extremely difficult to fight. The frame structure, reinforced with brick, burned liked tinder and soon was a roaring inferno."[144]

"The building, wooden, was an easy prey to the fire. The blazes crackled as they crept from one room to another, and even upward toward the roof. So bright was the blaze by this time that people in Phoebus and Hampton could see the glare, and crowds began to arrive in all manner of conveyances. They were halted at the bridge, and only those on foot could pass over."[145]

All guests would thankfully escape with their lives. A reported 20,000 spectators watched as the flames raged all night, leaving the landmark in smoldering ruins by the next morning.[146] Many guests that were displaced coming to hotels in Phoebus and the Old Soldiers' Home.[147]

"The fire could be seen as far away as Norfolk and Newport News," Quarstein says. "It was huge."[148]

---

[144] "Hotel Chamberlin Destroyed By Flames," *Daily Press* (March 8, 1920).

[145] Ibid.

[146] Mark St. John Erickson, "Hotel Chamberlin boosted Hampton resort's status" (Daily Press, March 8, 2018).

[147] "Famous Resort," *Daily Press* (March 8, 1920).

[148] Mark St. John Erickson, "Hotel Chamberlin boosted Hampton resort's status" (Daily Press, March 8, 2018).

JJJ – Firefighters and onlookers gather as the Chamberlin Hotel rages on March 7, 1920 (Daily Press).

KKK – The Chamberlin Fire on the evening of March 7, 1920 (Daily Press).

LLL – The Chamberlin Hotel is lost on March 7, 1920 (Daily Press).

MMM – The Chamberlin Hotel on fire on March 7, 1920 (Daily Press).

NNN – The remains of the Chamberlin Hotel (Hampton Public Library – Cheyne Collection).

OOO – The remains of the Chamberlin Hotel (Hampton Public Library – Cheyne

Collection).

PPP – The remains of the Chamberlin Hotel (Hampton Public Library – Cheyne Collection).

QQQ – The burned-out remains of the Chamberlin Hotel on March 8, 1920 (Daily Press).

RRR – The Chamberlin Hotel on March 8, 1920 (Daily Press).

SSS – The aftermath of the Chamberlin Fire on the morning of March 8, 1920 (Daily Press).

HOTEL CHAMBERLIN
DESTROYED BY FLAMES

TTT - Headline from March 8, 1920 (Daily Press).

UUU – The aftermath of the Chamberlin Fire on the morning of March 8, 1920 (Daily Press).

The Chamberlin Hotel manager George F. Adams would write a letter of appreciation to the Phoebus Fire Department in the Daily Press on March 19, 1920.[149] It read: "My Dear Sir – I am very glad indeed to write to you in expression of my appreciation of the wonderful work done by you and your men during the Chamberlin fire. We certainly owe the preservation of the laundry and power plant to the efforts of your company, and it is indeed a delight to so express our obligation. Very truly yours, George F. Adams."[150]

It would take eight years for the replacement to open. The Chamberlin-Vanderbilt Hotel as it was called in its early years is still in use as The Chamberlin and serves as a retirement community in 2019.

---

[149] "Phoebus Men Are Thanked for Fight," *Daily Press* (March 19, 1920).
[150] Ibid.

Chamberlin Work Nearing Completion

Above photo shows the Chamberlin, now under construction at Old Point Comfort, as it appeared a few days ago. The work on the new hostelry is progressing satisfactorily, officials say, and it is expected to be completed by April 1, the date set for the formal opening of the hotel.

VVV – Chamberlin Hotel under construction on October 19, 1927 (Daily Press).

WWW – The new Chamberlin-Vanderbilt, later just the Chamberlin Hotel in 1928. (Tim Receveur).

Pride of Phoebus Spotlight
Christopher Columbus (C.C.) Mugler

President of the Phoebus Fire Department
Phoebus Merchant from 1898-1942
Founder of the Bank of Phoebus
Life: 1869-1942

C. C. MUGLER

Christopher Columbus Mugler, or C.C. Mugler as he was known in Phoebus, was a well-respected merchant and civic leader, and served as the President of the Phoebus Fire Department in the first few decades of the 20th century. Mugler also served several terms as the President of the Virginia State Firemen's Association and was instrumental in bringing the state firemen's convention to Phoebus in 1930.

Today C.C. Mugler is best known as the founder of Mugler's men's clothing store which he founded in 1898. "For many years, Peninsula men have been convinced they can find almost anything at Mugler's even if it can't be found any place else,"[151] according to the *Daily Press* in 1979. The business would be sold by his son John P. Mugler to Tom Gear in 1970.[152]

Mugler was also the President of the Phoebus Chamber of Commerce and the Peninsular Chamber of Commerce in the 1920s and 1930s and was a founder of the Bank of Phoebus.

---

[151] Jim Wright, "Phoebus Keeps Best of Past with Today's Changes," *Daily Press* (October 14, 1979).
[152] Ibid.

XXX – Mugler clothing store at 28 East Mellen Street on April 2, 1900, the day that Phoebus became an incorporated town (Tom Mugler).

YYY – Looking north on Mallory Street in 1928. Mugler was one of the founders of the Bank of Phoebus, the white building on the left (Tim Receveur).

ZZZ – Robert's Antiques is currently operating in the building where C.C. Mugler ran his clothing store for decades (April Receveur).

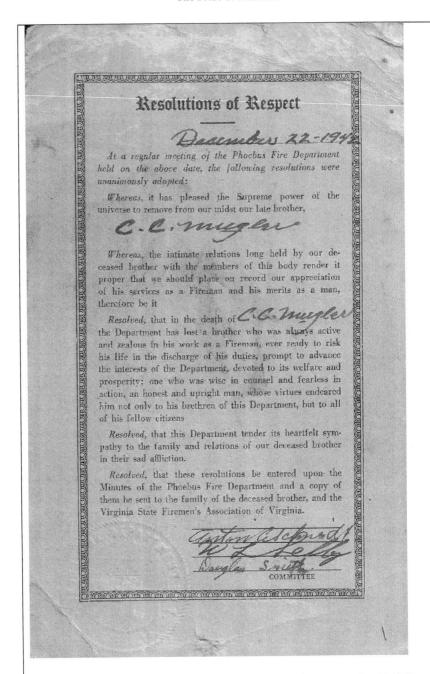

Resolutions of Respect

December 22-1942

At a regular meeting of the Phoebus Fire Department held on the above date, the following resolutions were unanimously adopted:

Whereas, it has pleased the Supreme power of the universe to remove from our midst our late brother,

C. C. Mugler

Whereas, the intimate relations long held by our deceased brother with the members of this body render it proper that we should place on record our appreciation of his services as a Fireman and his merits as a man, therefore be it

Resolved, that in the death of *C. C. Mugler* the Department has lost a brother who was always active and zealous in his work as a Fireman, ever ready to risk his life in the discharge of his duties, prompt to advance the interests of the Department, devoted to its welfare and prosperity; one who was wise in counsel and fearless in action, an honest and upright man, whose virtues endeared him not only to his brethren of this Department, but to all of his fellow citizens

Resolved, that this Department tender its heartfelt sympathy to the family and relations of our deceased brother in their sad affliction.

Resolved, that these resolutions be entered upon the Minutes of the Phoebus Fire Department and a copy of them be sent to the family of the deceased brother, and the Virginia State Firemen's Association of Virginia.

COMMITTEE

AAAA - Resolutions of Respect on the passing of C.C. Mugler in December 1942 (Tom Mugler).

5 COMMUNITY PRIDE:
1920 – 1940

The pride and respect that the community held for the Phoebus Fire
Department is captured in an article from January 25, 1920.

"One of the best organizations in Phoebus and the one, in which the
people of that growing town dote upon, is the Phoebus fire department, an
organization which has done more to advertise Phoebus than any other
single attraction. The department has won more state prizes than any other
volunteer organization in Virginia and it is a treat to visit the headquarters
of the department to look over the trophies which it has taken from the
various state conventions."[153]

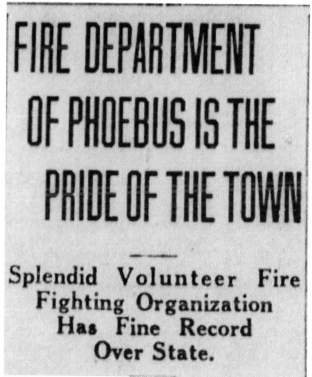

BBBB - Headline from January 25, 1920 (Daily Press).

---

[153] "Fire Department of Phoebus is the Pride of the Town," *Daily Press* (January 25,
1920).

"Recently the company was reorganized with a number of the best young men in the town as members. Captain George H. Lancer, the present chief and a charter member of the company, along with Secretary Edward C. Kaiser, he is entitled to the credit to again putting the fire department back into condition."[154]

"Several days ago, at the suggestion of the *Daily Press*, C. Ethelbert Cheyne, the Hampton photographer, arranged to take the picture of the department and its fine equipment and today the *Daily Press* is presenting that photograph to the people of Phoebus. Naturally many of the members are missing from the group, but as will be seen by looking over the photo, Phoebus has every reason for pointing with pride to this fine body of men. Fighting fires because of the desire to serve their town is the way the members of the department look upon their duties."[155]

"There are no paid firefighters in Phoebus except the man who remains at the station all the time and fills the position of Chief Engineer. This man is Chester A. Haas and his selection for the Important post was made by the company and confirmed by the Phoebus town council. Mr. Haas is exceptionally well qualified for his duties. The worth of the Phoebus volunteer firemen to Phoebus cannot be estimated in dollars and cents. Every year the firemen save hundreds of dollars' worth of property, but the advertising the department gives to Phoebus is worth many times what It saves from fire losses. By having such a department, the property owners of Phoebus are saved considerable money in fire, insurance rates, while the citizens are permitted to rest secure that they are protected at all times again."[156]

CCCC - Scene at the Phoebus train station on August 22, 1924 (Tom Jackson).

The pride and respect from the community was also on full display in a photo and story from a homecoming in August 1924. The department had

---

[154] "Fire Department of Phoebus is the Pride of the Town," *Daily Press* (January 25, 1920).
[155] Ibid.
[156] Ibid.

just returned from the yearly Virginia State Firemen's Association convention in Harrisonburg, Virginia. Phoebus would win the top prize for the best company without a band and the town would turn out to congratulate them.

PHOEBUS FIREMEN GET ROYAL WELCOME HOME LAST NIGHT

People of the Town, Headed by National Soldiers' Home Turned Out to Greet Winners Harrisonburg Prize.

DDDD - Headline on August 23, 1924 (Daily Press).

Here is how the welcome home was covered in the Daily Press on August 23, 1924:

"Practically all the people In Phoebus were at the Chesapeake and Ohio station last night to welcome the members of the Phoebus fire department back home after capturing the prize for being the best appearing company in the state firemen's parade in Harrisonburg on Thursday."[157]

"The returning firemen were showered with congratulations from the people at home, while the sirens and whistles made a noise that would have brought joy to most any occasion. As the firemen marched through the streets to the engine house the citizens, lined up along them, cheered the victors freely and the town gave the laddies a welcome back home which must have done everyone in the party good."[158]

"Mayor William J. Kearney, who got up the reception for the homecoming of the firemen, headed the parade and marched at the head of the department, with Chief George H. Lancer leading his men. After passing alone Mallory street to Mellen to Chesapeake Avenue and to the engine house, the firemen came to a halt at the building where the committee had arranged a fine spread of sandwiches, cool drinks and ice cream."[159]

"The engine house was gaily decorated and the home-coming of the

---

[157] "Phoebus Firemen Get Royal Welcome Home Last Night," *Daily Press* (August 24, 1924).
[158] Ibid.
[159] Ibid.

winning department was in every way an appreciation of the people of the town for the good deportment of the men in Harrisonburg and the fact that Phoebus came out victorious as the best company in line without a band."[160]

"The firemen were deeply impressed by the reception they received, while the people of Phoebus evinced a keen interest in the men who day in and night in are ready and willing at all hours to respond to the call to save the homes in the town from destruction by fire. The firemen said they were glad to be back home and the Phoebus folks showed them they were glad to have them back, as well as elated over the honors won by them."[161]

"In the firemen's party from Phoebus at Harrisonburg were Chief George H. Lancer, Engineer Chester Haas, Anton Schmidt, N. H. Peach, Leon Sherman, Robert Miller, Amil Unlauft, W. E. Lancer, Robert Gammon, Edward Kaiser, C. C. Mugler, E. L. Clarke, Andrew Mittermaier, John Kaiser, John Byrnes, Jesse Lewis, Samuel Fuller, Horace Mingee, Jack Mingee, William C. Mingee. M. Joinvllle, Charles H. Warren, John Schaub, Edward Dore, Hugh Loughran, John Mittermaier and W. L. Selby."[162]

Here's a look at that panoramic photo in sections:

---

[160] "Phoebus Firemen Get Royal Welcome Home Last Night," *Daily Press* (August 24, 1924).
[161] Ibid.
[162] Ibid.

EEEE- Scene at the Phoebus train station on August 22, 1924 (Tom Jackson).

FFFF - Scene at the Phoebus train station on August 22, 1924 (Tom Jackson).

GGGG - Scene at the Phoebus train station on August 22, 1924 (Tom Jackson).

HHHH - Scene at the Phoebus train station on August 22, 1924 (Tom Jackson).

IIII - Scene at the Phoebus train station on August 22, 1924 (Tom Jackson).

JJJJ - Scene at the Phoebus train station on August 22, 1924 (Tom Jackson).

KKKK - Scene at the Phoebus train station on August 22, 1924 (Tom Jackson).

American LaFrance Triple Combination Pumper

In 1924, the Volunteer Fire Department purchased an American LaFrance Triple Combination Pumper for $12,750, which was used until the late

1950's when it was sold to the Virginia Beach Fire Department. After it was retired from service, it was purchased by a retired Virginia Beach Firefighter and it has stayed in that family. The engine was completely restored by the current owner and has occasionally ventured back to Phoebus: most notably during the Phoebus Days parade.[163]

LLLL - American LaFrance Triple Combination Pumper (Tom Jackson).

MMMM - The Firemen ready for a parade around 1927 (Tom Jackson).

---

[163] "History of the Phoebus Volunteer Fire Department," *Phoebus Volunteer Fire Department* (2019), 4.

NNNN – Preparing for a parade around 1930 (Tom Jackson).

OOOO - Fire Department in 1937 (Library of Virginia).

Phoebus Hosts State Firemen's Convention

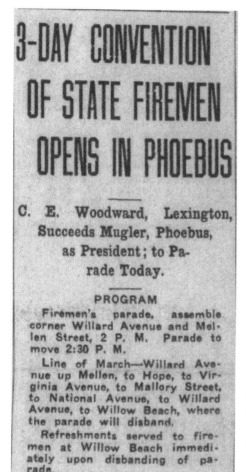

3-DAY CONVENTION OF STATE FIREMEN OPENS IN PHOEBUS

C. E. Woodward, Lexington, Succeeds Mugler, Phoebus, as President; to Parade Today.

PROGRAM

Firemen's parade, assemble corner Willard Avenue and Mellen Street, 2 P. M. Parade to move 2:30 P. M.

Line of March—Willard Avenue up Mellen, to Hope, to Virginia Avenue, to Mallory Street, to National Avenue, to Willard Avenue, to Willow Beach, where the parade will disband.

Refreshments served to firemen at Willow Beach immediately upon disbanding of parade.

1930 was a banner year in Phoebus as the Virginia State Firemen's Association hosted its 44th annual convention in town.

This is how Phoebus looked on August 27, 1930: "Phoebus is beautifully decorated and at the approach to the town from Hampton there is a large banner reading "Welcome Firemen," and another at the Old Point reservation bridge. Firemen were coming in on all trains and by automobile yesterday and last night."[164]

The convention started with a welcoming ceremony in the American Theatre, which was decorated accordingly for the visitors. The firemen were given the keys to the town of Phoebus and told that they were expected to enjoy themselves during their three days on the Peninsula and in Phoebus.[165]

"The volunteer firemen were commended highly for their bravery, their service to the state and their communities, and their earnest desire to prevent fires, in the addresses of those who welcomed them to Phoebus. It was shortly after 10 o'clock when President C. C. Mugler announced that the convention would come to order. Mr. Mugler, with a few appropriate remarks, introduced City Attorney Percy Carmel, of Phoebus, who presided at the welcoming

---

[164] "Forty-First Convention Virginia Firemen to Open in Phoebus Today," *Daily Press* (August 27, 1930).

[165] "3-Day Convention of State Firemen Opens in Phoebus," *Daily Press* (August 28, 1930).

exercises. Mr. Carmel declared that he was particularly happy to preside at' the session and then introduced Frank A. Kearney, Jr one of the leading attorneys of the, lower end of the peninsula, who forcefully, welcomed the visiting firemen to Phoebus and the lower end of the Virginia peninsula."[166] Frank A. Kearney, Jr. was the son of Chief Frank A. Kearney who died in the Spanish Flu Epidemic of 1918.

"Mr. Kearney said that Phoebus has been a member of the state association for many years and declared that the officials of the town, its people and everyone connected with Phoebus felt a keen pleasure upon having the firemen come to them for the 44th annual convention. He called attention to the attractions around here, including the National Soldiers' Home, Fort Monroe, Langley Field, Hampton and Newport News and expressed the wish that the stay of the firemen would be such that all would want to come back to Phoebus again."[167]

Kearney praised the firemen for their work and paid a high tribute to the Phoebus fire department for its services to Phoebus, Mr. Kearney closed by presenting the key to Phoebus to President C.C. Mugler on behalf of Mayor William J. Kearney, who was prevented from being present at the opening exercises, due to slight indisposition.

State Senator Frank B. Ball, of Alexandria, said that he was happy to be in Phoebus and was sure that each fireman felt the same way."[168]

PPPP - Fire Department in 1930 (Tom Jackson).

---

[166] "3-Day Convention of State Firemen Opens in Phoebus," *Daily Press* (August 28, 1930).
[167] Ibid.
[168] Ibid.

QQQQ - 1930 Virginia State Firemen's Association Book from 1930 (Tom Jackson).

RRRR - Fire Department in 1930 (Tom Jackson).

SSSS - The Phoebus Fire Department around 1930 (Tony Schmidt).

TTTT - Phoebus Fire Department in 1930 (Tom Jackson).

UUUU - Phoebus Fire Department in 1930 (Tom Jackson).

Phoebus Fire Department No. 1

On Tuesday evening, February 9th, 1926, will be Roll Call Night.

On Tuesday evening, February 23rd, 1926, will be a regular meeting and business of importance. Every member of the Department is expected to attend this meeting.

The Phoebus Fire Department has levied two assessments against you during the year of 1925. This applies to each and every member of the Department. These assessments and dues must be paid on the ninth day of March, in order that the Secretary cand sen your name in to the Clerk of the Courts to be EXEMPT from jury duty.

Please send your check to the Secretary, if you are in arrears.

Every member of the Department is a partner to *its success. Are you loafing on your job?*

The Department has had a very successful year, and just let us make this a banner year for the Phoebus Fire Department.

My books show your account to be as follows:

For Dues.. $ 1.25

For Assessments............................... $ 2.00

Fraternally yours,

E. C. KAISER, Secretary

VVVV - Bill for Fire Department dues in 1926 (Tony Schmidt).

Complete Formation For Firemen's Parade

First division, forming on Willard Avenue facing Mellen Street: State police, Phoebus police, officials of Phoebus, chief marshal, and aide, Fort Monroe band, Phoebus Fire Department and equipment, Fort Monroe firemen, Orange firemen, Orange Ladies' Auxiliary, Lexington firemen, Farmville firemen.

Second division, forming on Willard Avenue, rear first division: Marshal, Charlottesville band, Charlottesville Fire Department, Charlottesville Ladies' Auxiliary, Wythe Fire Department and equipment, Covington Fire Department, Harrisonburg Fire Department, Harrisonburg Ladies' Auxiliary, Culpeper Fire Department.

Third division forming on Willard Avenue: Marshal, city officials of Hampton, Langley Field band, Hampton Fire Department and apparatus, Langley Fire Department, Waynesboro firemen, Pulaski firemen, Bristol Firemen.

Fourth division forming on Segar Street, facing Willard Avenue: Marshal, Alexandria band, Alexandria firemen, Alexanderia Ladies' Auxiliary, Hot Springs firemen, Clifton Forge firemen, Gordonsville firemen.

Fifth division forming on Armistead Street, facing Willard Avenue: Marshal, Newport News Fireman's band, Newport News firemen, Newport News Ladies' Auxiliary, Fredericksburg firemen, Staunton firemen, Staunton Ladies' Auxiliary, Strausburg firemen, Winchester firemen.

Sixth division forming on Howard Street, facing Wihard Avenue: Luray firemen, Crozet firemen, Jefferson firemen, Jefferson Ladies' Auxiliary.

Seventh division forming on Willard avenue: All floats and automobiles entering the contest for prize. Marshal will be: Joseph E. Carpenter, Norman Turner, Jean Cooney, Paige Fitchett, Capt. Taylor C. Holtzclaw, Henry Malone, and William Ashburn.

WWWW - Parade setup in Phoebus for the 1930 Virginia Firemen's Association convention (Daily Press).

PHOEBUS FIRE DEPARTMENT No. 1

The motto of the Phoebus Fire Department is: "For the People's Good". The Department was organized in January, 1893, and today it is one of the best volunteer fire organizations in the State of Virginia. The Fire Department of Phoebus boasts of having an American LaFrance steamer, a Mack combination hose and chemical truck with a 35-foot extension ladder and a modern up-to-date 750-gallon American LaFrance pumping engine.

XXXX - Clip about the Phoebus Fire Department in 1930 (Martha Morris).

Chief Schmidt Takes Over

On December 6, 1930, a letter arrived to the fire station from North Charleston, S.C. It was from Chief George H. Lancer, who had been in charge of the Phoebus Fire Department since the death of Chief Frank A.

Kearney in the Spanish flu outbreak in 1918. The letter read:

To the Officers and Members of the Phoebus Fire Department.

Dear Sirs – I hereby tender my resignation as chief of the Phoebus Fire Department, to take effect when my successor is elected. My reason for resigning is due to the fact that I will not be able to come back to Phoebus for two years or more, as my present work will keep me here that length of time. Boys, I wish you all a Merry Christmas and a Happy New Year. Wish I could be with you always, you smoke eaters.

Your chief, George H. Lancer."[169]

1931 would start a new era that would continue until 1963 when Anton Alexander Schmidt would complete his ascension from lantern boy to Chief of the Phoebus Fire Department.

"A.A. Schmidt was last night elected the chief of the Phoebus Fire Department, to succeed Captain George H. Lancer, who resigned several weeks ago, due to the fact that he is at present employed in Charleston, S.C.

The election of officers for the coming year occupied the main portion of the business session of the firemen last night, and the members also enjoyed one of those famous baked bean dinners served by Station Master Chester Haas. During the banquet several of the members made short talks and the new chief was pledged the hearty cooperation of all the firemen in the Phoebus department."[170] The officers elected are: Chief – A.A. Schmidt; First Assistant Chief – E.L. Clarke; Second Assistant Chief – W.L. Selby; President – C.C. Mugler; Foreman – R.F. Snow; First Assistant Foreman – William E. Lancer; Second Assistant Foreman – T.A. Stacey; Secretary – E.C. Kaiser; Statistician – John Mittlemaier; Chaplain – Rev. Arthur Machen Lewis; Physician – Dr. O.W. Ward; and Station Master – Chester A. Haas.[171]

---

[169] Letter from George H. Lancer, (December 6, 1930).
[170] "Schmidt is Chief Phoebus Firemen for Coming Year," *Daily Press* (January 13, 1931).
[171] Ibid.

Pride of Phoebus Spotlight
Ernest Lancer (E.L.) Clarke
Longest Serving Member of the Phoebus Fire Department (73 years)
Phoebus Merchant from 1915-1987
Life: 1892-1987

Ernest Lancer Clarke was better known as E.L. Clarke and has the distinction of being the longest serving member of the Phoebus Fire Department, having served from 1914 until his death in 1987, some 73 years.

Ernest was born on September 13, 1892 in Alexandria, Virginia, but due to an outbreak of a deadly disease there, the Clarke family moved to Phoebus in 1894, where Ernest lived the rest of his life. Captain George Lancer and William Lancer were his uncles, so Ernest spent his youth at the Phoebus Fire Department.

YYYY - Fig 1. Ernest Clarke, as a young boy, is sitting on top of the fire wheel. His uncle, William Lancer, is pictured to the far left holding the rope (Tom Jackson).

Today, Ernest is remembered for being the owner of E.L. Clarke

Fashions for Men, Phoebus, for 70 years. The sign still hangs on Mellen Street in 2019.

Ernest attended Phoebus Graded School. In the photo to the left Ernest Clarke is the young boy sitting in the front holding a bugle with his uncle George Lancer sitting to his right. Following graduation, he attended Virginia Tech and was a Navy veteran of World War I. He joined the Phoebus Fire Department on April 18, 1914, at the age of 21. He was soon promoted from lantern boy (LB) to fireman. Over time he worked his way to Lieutenant.

He was a former director of Bank of Phoebus and a former member of Phoebus Town Council.

ZZZZ - Officers of the Phoebus Fire Department. Ernest Clarke is the fourth from the left, holding the middle trumpet. CC Mugler is the second from the left and future Chief A.A. Schmidt is holding the trumpet on the right (Tom Jackson).

6 A NEW ERA:
1938

By the late 1930s the fire department was outgrowing their original fire station that had been designed for horse-pulled equipment in 1893 for a meager $694. The United States was deep into the Great Depression and these two things would come together to modernize the Phoebus Fire Department in 1938.

During the Great Depression, Franklin D. Roosevelt's New Deal brought jobs and construction to Phoebus with its Civilian Conservation Corps (CCC) and Works Progress Administration (WPA) programs to provide unemployment relief and to improve public facilities. The WPA began in 1935, and by the end of its run in 1943, almost every community in the United States had a new park, bridge, or school that was constructed by the program. Through the program, the U.S. government would match 45 cents for each dollar spent.[172]

AAAAA - Mellen Street 1936, (Hampton Public Library - Cheyne Collection).

In 1936 Mayor Kearney began soliciting ideas from the Town Council for projects in Phoebus. Kearney suggested the necessity for a new town hall,

---

[172] "Works Progress Administration (WPA)," *History* (A&E Television Networks: August 21, 2018), https://www.history.com/topics/great-depression/works-progress-administration.

Councilman R.F. Snow stated the need for a modern fire house, postmaster John P. Mugler stressed the need for a new post office, and Councilman Alvin Scott proposed public playgrounds. Other suggestions were made, including a complete curbing plan for the town.

The New Deal programs helped build the post office, fire department, school, and water tower in Phoebus. In the Hampton area, these programs helped rebuild the Fort Monroe bandshell that was destroyed by the hurricane and construct the High Speed Wind Tunnel at Langley Research Center, along with Aberdeen Gardens, Hampton's old City Hall, the Buckroe water tower, and more.

On August 11, 1938, Mayor Kearney appealed to the citizens of Phoebus in 1936 to vote yes on a $40,000 bond referendum "for the erection of a new Town Hall and Fire Department, at a cost to the town of $20,714.75, repairs to hard surfaced streets and pouring additional streets; additional curbs and gutters, at a cost to the town of $13,062.75 and installing new sewers in those portions of town not now sewered, at a cost to the town of $6,222.50."[173]

Adding, "be it remembered that the WPA will grant the town a free gift of 45¢ for each dollar the town expends, up to and not exceeding $31,909.00; so that the two funds will provide $71,909.00 [$1.29 million in 2018 when adjusted for inflation], a sum estimated to be sufficient to complete both projects.[174] Be it also remembered that the Town today has only a bonded indebtedness (other than for school purposes) of $21,000, which is practically nothing. The town at one time had $50,000 bonded indebtedness, which was retired promptly. Besides, most of this money which would be spent right here in Phoebus, giving our men employment and stimulating business for our merchants, which would be especially beneficial to every one of our people."[175]

Big Decisions

The task of the new building for the fire department was assigned to Chief Anton Alexander (A.A.) Schmidt. Better known as Tony, Chief Schmidt would look for possible new locations and a design for the new building. Although the initial plans had the location remaining the same, Schmidt had other ideas like moving it to Mellen Street near the American Theatre. It

---

[173] "To The Voters of Phoebus, VA," *Daily Press* (August 11, 1938).
[174] Ibid.
[175] Ibid.

was discussed that this location could provide more space and allow the new trucks to come in from the back and pull through instead of always backing in. Designs were studied around the state and Chief Schmidt paid a visit to the Chincoteague Fire Station in 1938 which would serve as the model for the new building.

BBBBB - The Phoebus Fire Department copied the Chincoteague Fire Station.

CCCCC - Chief Schmidt visiting the Chincoteague Fire Department in early 1938 (Tony Schmidt).

In the end, the new structure would be built on the same location as the original Fireman's Hall. In February, the initial estimates came in at $21,000 and Phoebus had a series of fundraisers including a Firemen's Ball to raise money for the new structure.[176]

FIRE DEPARTMENT IN PHOEBUS PLANS $21,000 BUILDING

Funds Realized by Dance Wednesday to Aid in Paying For Two-Story Brick Structure

"The Phoebus Fire Department will sponsor a dance, February 18 in the Hampton Armory on North King Street. The decision to hold the dance was reached at a recent meeting of the department and funds will be devoted to a building program which has long been under consideration. The present department quarters are old and constructed of wood and for some time 'smoke-eaters' have been considering ways and means of obtaining money to erect a new engine house. Chairman of the dance committee is John Mittlemaier and Ed Kaiser is in charge of ticket sales. Other members of the committee are: William Kuss. W. L. Selbv and John Mugler. Music for the affair will be furnished by the Jolly Jazz Orchestra

---

[176] "Phoebus Firemen To Give Benefit Dance in Armory," *Daily Press* (January 26, 1938).

beginning at 9:30p.m."[177]

DDDDD - Ad for the Firemen's Ball on the February 16, 1938 (Daily Press).

As the year progressed the cost and function of the building changed slightly. It was decided that the Phoebus Municipal Building also known as the new Town Hall would also be constructed under the same WPA program at the same time. The building would sit adjacent to the Fire Department. There is still a plaque that reads "Phoebus VA Town Hall 1938" on the old Town Hall building today.

The price of the building went up to between $30,000 and $35,000. It was decided to elevate the walls of the town hall building two more feet to get an appearance of greater height. The committee said that people had complained that the building as proposed looked "too squatty."[178]

Another proposal made to the building committee that the town hall be raised to two stories, was rejected flatly by the councilmen who pointed out that costs would be too prohibitive, and the space of the additional story was not needed. A "purpose for which it could be utilized, they said, was not known."[179] In the end, the Harwood Construction Company of Newport News built the two buildings for $35,500.[180]

There were notices in the papers in August and September 1938 asking

---

[177] "Phoebus Firemen To Give Benefit Dance in Armory," *Daily Press* (January 26, 1938).
[178] "To Explain to Voters," *Daily Press* (August 3, 1938).
[179] Ibid.
[180] "Work on City Halls in Hampton, Phoebus Progresses," *Daily Press* (October 2, 1938).

people for bids for the Town Hall and the Fire Department buildings. There are no reports of who bought the buildings, but photos from October 2, 1938 appear to show the Town Hall building being demolished.

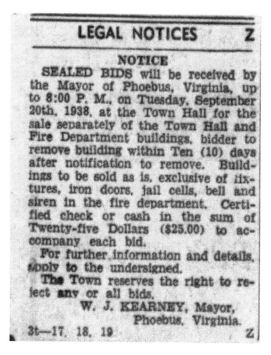

LEGAL NOTICES   Z

NOTICE

SEALED BIDS will be received by the Mayor of Phoebus, Virginia, up to 8:00 P. M., on Tuesday, September 20th, 1938, at the Town Hall for the sale separately of the Town Hall and Fire Department buildings, bidder to remove building within Ten (10) days after notification to remove. Buildings to be sold as is, exclusive of fixtures, iron doors, jail cells, bell and siren in the fire department. Certified check or cash in the sum of Twenty-five Dollars ($25.00) to accompany each bid.

For further information and details, apply to the undersigned.

The Town reserves the right to reject any or all bids.

W. J. KEARNEY, Mayor,
Phoebus, Virginia.

3t—17, 18, 19   Z

EEEEE - Notice from September 16, 1938 (Daily Press).

FFFFF - Phoebus Town Hall being demolished to make way for the new Fire Department and Town Hall in October 1938 (Daily Press).

A New Era

Demolition and construction would continue throughout October and November 1938. The cornerstones of the Fire Department and the Town Hall were laid on November 15, 1938 and approximately 200 citizens showed up for the dedication. Both cornerstones enclose copper containers that included artifacts from Phoebus to be preserved for posterity.[181]

GGGGG - *Members of the Fire Department prepare to place the cornerstone In the new building. They are, left to right: Charles H. Warren, John Boyhan, C. C. Mugler, and Ollie Freeburger, four of the oldest members, and C.C. Kraft (Daily Press).*

New Town Fire Department Culminates Dream Fostered 40 Years Ago In Phoebus

HHHHH - *New Town Fire Department Culminates Dream Fostered 40 Years Ago in Phoebus – November 20, 1938 – (Daily Press).*

---

[181] "Impressive Rites Feature Laying of 2 Cornerstones," *Daily Press* (November 16, 1938).

Members of Phoebus Fire Department and Town Council attended the dedication and the four oldest members of the Fire Department were chosen to lay the cornerstone. They were Charles H. Warren, John Boyhan, C. C. Mugler, and Ollie Freeburger. The cornerstone for the new Town Hall was laid by A.A. Kraft, John Mittlemaier, Edward Camnitz, W. H. Graham, and Robert Snow, councilmen and Mayor William J. Kearney.

IIIII - The cornerstone for the new Town Hall was laid by A.A. Kraft, John Mittlemaier, Edward Camnitz, W. H. Graham, and Robert Snow, councilmen and Mayor William J. Kearney.

Mayor William J. Kearney was present and gave some brief remarks, but the day is remembered for the speech by Judge Percy Carmel, the town attorney, that day.[182] Carmel declared that the "Phoebus Fire Department was closely associated with the town of Phoebus and the town's growth and forwardness."

Continuing, he said that "before the town of Phoebus became a municipality, the fire department was organized. The need of a thriving, rapidly growing community for protection against the hazards of fire was apparent. So the best citizens of what was then a sparsely settled, unincorporated community with only a few small badly built wooden buildings, banded themselves together and more than 40 years ago formed

---

[182] "Impressive Rites Feature Laying of 2 Cornerstones," *Daily Press* (November 16, 1938).

the Phoebus fire department."[183]

Here is Judge Carmel's speech from that day:

"The membership consisted of the best citizens in the town, social position, financial responsibility and business distinction was of little moment when this organization was formed. The membership consisted of lawyers, doctors, mechanics, tradesman, and laborers. A man's religion, or creed, or position in the community was not considered. A more democratic and cosmopolitan organization was not imaginable. A more active organization had never existed."[184]

"Every worthwhile movement in the town of Phoebus since the organization of the Phoebus fire department found the fire department in the front ranks fighting for not only the betterment of the fire department, but of the community in which it was a part. The membership of the Phoebus fire department had a most active part in the creation and incorporation of the town of Phoebus."[185]

"In almost every community there is some outstanding fraternal, social, or civic organization that gives prominence and favorable publicity to the community in which is located. With us it has been the Phoebus Fire Department. It contains the virtues and characteristics of an outstanding fraternal, social, and civic organization."[186]

"No needy citizen, whether a member of the department or not, has ever appealed for help and had his appeal gone unheeded. No Memorial Day has ever gone by since this department has been in existence and failed to find the members of this department visiting the graves of departed members and placing thereon flowers and an American flag in memory of those that had been members in life. Once each year a public memorial service is held in honor of the deceased members."[187]

"The families of the departed members are cared for as tenderly and completely as the finances of the department will permit. No fraternal or

---

[183] "New Town Fire Department Culminates Dream Fostered 40 Years Ago in Phoebus," *Daily Press* (November 20, 1938).
[184] Ibid.
[185] Ibid.
[186] Ibid.
[187] Ibid.

social organization could do more. In matters affecting the public good and public interest, the fire department and the members thereof have taken an active and wholehearted interest."[188]

"The Phoebus fire department started off in an unsightly frame building, with poor and insufficient equipment and the growth of the department has kept pace with the growth of the town. As the town grew, the department grew. Better equipment was procured, in order that more efficient service could be rendered, and the most advanced methods of firefighting and fire prevention was employed and studied in order that this department would be second to none in the State in the matter of fire prevention and in firefighting."[189]

"Now we lay the cornerstone for a fine, new, modern brick building; the new home of the fire department, to replace the old antiquated one, where we kept valuable equipment in facilities little more than a shed. In this world in which we lived, either we go ahead or go backwards. Some people and some organizations are content to live in the past and to spend their time recalling memories and events of years ago. But not so with the Phoebus Fire Department."[190]

"The history of the Phoebus Fire Department is rich and honorable, in service and achievement. The records record service after service rendered to the community by its deportment and bearing in Virginia conventions and in visits to cities beyond the borders of this State. They have ornaments and prizes won in gallant competition with other splendid departments throughout the State, though in competition with larger communities."[191]

"But this department is not content to live in the past. Erection of this new building is conclusively showing that the Phoebus Fire Department occupies the high place in this community for which it has been known from the time of its existence."[192]

"Its members are just as fine and its leadership just as splendid and just as capable as it has ever ben; having continued on this high plane for more

---

[188188] "New Town Fire Department Culminates Dream Fostered 40 Years Ago in Phoebus," *Daily Press* (November 20, 1938).
[189] Ibid.
[190] Ibid.
[191] Ibid.
[192] Ibid.

than 40 years. Tell me, if you can, of any organization whose membership is more unselfish, more loyal, or more patriotic. The members get no pay for their services. On the contrary they pay dues to the organization, in order to carry on the work that they have laid out. Yet no fire is too big for them to risk their safety and lives for the protection of the property and lives of others. No night too dark nor weather too bad for them to fall to heed the call to duty."[193]

"And now when the time comes to erect a new fire house and home they went into their own treasury and furnished a substantial part of the cost in order that the construction of this building be possible; even as they have in the past purchased some equipment from their own funds, which they might have used for entertainment, trips and other pleasures. My wish then for the future is: That you continue the fine work of service and devotion to duty that you have setup by past performance and if this be done the future for the department, the town of Phoebus, and the surrounding community, is bright. We have laid here today the cornerstone of a beautiful building, but you need not have done this to establish yourself in the hearts of the town people or to remind them of services rendered. By your unselfish services to the town and to the surrounding community in general."[194]

"You have built a monument greater than the finest of marble and stone. A shaft that will last until ages have passed and time shall have withered and gone."[195]

In addition to the new Fire Department and Town Hall, the new campus included the police and jail. It was also the Mayor's office until the consolidation with Hampton in 1952.

With a modern Fire Department in place, Phoebus could upgrade its equipment and provide even better service to the community. In 1940 Phoebus received a special delivery. William Toch, a delivery engineer, drove a new Diamond T fire truck from the Detroit factory of the General Fire Truck corporation to Phoebus. The truck cost around $5,000 and was powered by a 95 horsepower Hercules engine, and was equipped with a 200-gallon booster pump and a 500-gallon centrifugal two-stage pump. It

---

[193] "New Town Fire Department Culminates Dream Fostered 40 Years Ago in Phoebus," *Daily Press* (November 20, 1938).
[194] Ibid.
[195] Ibid.

carried 1,200 feet of two-and-a-half-inch hose, as well as a quantity of three-inch hose for the booster tank.[196]

The truck was bought to not only to provide better service to Phoebus but also to provide new coverage to the Chesapeake district. Hampton withdrew from the county as a magisterial district in 1940 and was no longer answering fire calls. Phoebus had the staff to support the Chesapeake district of Elizabeth City County and agreed to provide support with this additional truck.[197]

JJJJJ - Phoebus Fire Station, Police Station, and Town Hall around 1940.

Ghosts at the Fire Department?

With over 125 years of history on one spot, it's not hard to believe that there's been reports of ghosts over the years. The most famous is "Fire Engine Charlie" who supposedly walks the floors of the Phoebus Fire Department at night. "He can be heard walking the halls, and he likes to play pool in the wee hours of morning."[198]

---

[196] "New Fire Engine Arrives For Use By Town Firemen," *Daily Press* (May 12, 1940).

[197] Ibid.

[198] Jane Keane Polonsky and Joan McFarland Drum, *Hampton's Haunted Houses & How to Feed a Ghost* (Hampton, VA: Affordable Printing & Copies, Inc., 1998), 38.

KKKKK - Joseph Craigs, Phoebus Chief of Police, in 1938 (Dinah Balthis).

LLLLL - Mayor Kearney makes the first direct dialed number from his office in Phoebus on May 11, 1940. He dialed Mayor James V. Bickford of Hampton (Daily Press).

Pride of Phoebus Spotlight
Robert F. Snow
Phoebus Mayor (1941-1948)
Phoebus Town Council
Lifetime Member Phoebus Fire Department
Life: 1889-1948

Robert F. Snow was once the Mayor of Phoebus, a member of the Town Council, and a lifetime member of the Phoebus Fire Department, but today he is mainly remembered for the bicycle shop that he started in 1908 and that still bears his name today in Phoebus.

He was appointed to the Phoebus Town Council in 1914, at the age of 23, and had been active in municipal affairs until the time of his death. Elected mayor in 1942 following the death of Mayor William J. Kearney, he was re-elected in 1947 to serve a four-year term but died suddenly a year later.

Mayor Snow was a lifetime member of the Phoebus Fire Department which he joined in 1912. In 1921 he was appointed foreman, a position he held until 1947 when the pressure of his other duties forced him to resign.

This is how the city of Newport News recognized him following his death:

"Mayor Robert Franklin Snow was a pioneer citizen of the Peninsula and had been active in municipal affairs since he was 23 years of age. Mayor Robert Franklin Snow was a sterling example of a devoted public servant. He was a good neighbor and a loyal friend. The Peninsula of Virginia has lost a distinguished citizen whose name will long be remembered."[199]

MMMMM - Robert F. Snow Bicycle Shop around 1915 (Phoebus Memories).

NNNNN - Robert F. Snow's fire helmet – Gift from K. Sylvia Snow (Courtesy of the Hampton History Museum – ID: 2018.19.1).

---

[199] "Council of NN Commends the Life of Late Mayor Snow," *Daily Press* (October 15, 1948).

7 WORLD WAR II AND THE FIRST AID SQUAD: 1941-1951

As the 1940s started the United States found itself thrust into World War II. The Fire Department paid a very high price with members losing sons and brothers with names like Englebert, Fuller, and Ferris. In all 15 members of the Phoebus Fire Department fought in the war.[200]

A plaque hangs at the Town Hall building honoring the men who made the ultimate sacrifice during World War II. They are James Bradley, Johnnie Crabb, John B. Davenport, Jr., Jack Englebert, John D. Ferris, Wendall E. Fuller, Frank Hoak, Arthur G. Jenkins, James O'Leary, John E. Rhea, Willie Richardson, and George W. Sutterfield.

OOOOO - A plaque honoring Phoebus men who died in WWII.

Phoebus also prepared itself in case of an attack from Axis forces. On September 19, 1943, Mayor Snow joined the Fire Department to test new fire equipment near present day Interstate 64 in case of a German air raid.

---

[200] "Phoebus Fire Department Observes 50th Anniversary," *Daily Press* (January 14, 1943).

Life in Phoebus obviously went on during the war and the Fire Department recognized its 50th anniversary in January 1943. John P. Mugler, the Phoebus Postmaster and son of the late C.C. Mugler, was the toastmaster for the event. The event was attended by 60 guests from across the region. The only charter member who was able to make this remembrance was former Fire Chief George A. Lancer. In all, there were 80 members of the Fire Department in 1943.[201]

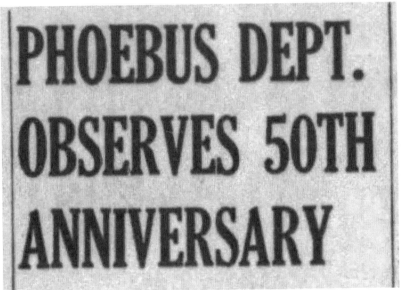

PPPPP - Headline from January 14, 1943 (Daily Press).

The Phoebus Volunteer Rescue Squad

Before the formation of the Phoebus Volunteer Rescue Squad, ambulance service to Phoebus was provided by the Wythe Fire Company and Dixie Hospital, which was located near what is now Hampton University. The hospital tried for years to get the Phoebus Fire Company to take over this responsibility. After a mysterious fire destroyed the Dixie Hospital ambulance, Phoebus was left with only one ambulance which was in Wythe. Responding to the need, the Phoebus First Aid Squad was formed. Ray Mingee remembers that volunteers called to the station quickly learned that

---

[201] "Phoebus Fire Department Observes 50th Anniversary," *Daily Press* (January 14, 1943).

"a little siren meant rescue services, and a big siren meant fire."[202] The Phoebus Fire Department would receive 200 alarms in 1945, 72 of the alarms would take place in Phoebus with 128 taking place in the Chesapeake district of Elizabeth City County which Phoebus took over from Hampton in 1940.[203]

QQQQQ - *Phoebus Fire Department March 9, 1947 (Library of Virginia - Cheyne Collection).*

Of the 200 alarms received by the Phoebus Fire Department during 1945, 11 were of an unknown cause, one was arson, 24 were false alarms, 16 were caused by cigarettes, 12 were short circuits, 18 were defective flues, 13 were automobile fires, 63 were grass fires, carelessness caused one fire, ten were forest fires, six were smoke scares, ten calls were trash fires, three were chimney fires, two were on boats, and six were oil stove explosions.[204]

---

[202] "Rescue Squad," *Daily Press* (August 9, 2012).
[203] "Phoebus Fire Boys Get 200 Calls in '45," *Daily Press* (January 6, 1946).
[204] Ibid.

By 1951, that number would balloon to 741 calls.[205] The largest portion of these calls (565) would consist of ambulance calls while just 176 would be fire alarms. Of the fire alarms, 74 would be in the Phoebus town limits, while the rest would be in the Chesapeake district of Elizabeth City County.[206]

The combination of supporting the Chesapeake district and ambulance runs required additional resources and, in 1947, a new Cadillac ambulance was purchased for Phoebus by the Chesapeake district.[207] The new ambulance cost $7099 according to Mayor Snow.

RRRRR - The new 1947 Cadillac ambulance. Mayor Snow announced that it cost the town $7,099 in November 1947 (Hampton Public Library).

In 1947 there was also a big push to train members of the Fire Department to not only administer first aid, but to also train others as first aid instructors. Members of the first aid squads of the Buckroe, Phoebus and Wythe took the course in November 1947 given by the American Red Cross at the Phoebus Fire Department. It led to a weekly in first aid fundamentals training on Monday nights in the late 1940s at the fire station.

---

[205] "Phoebus Fire Dept. Had 741 Calls in '51, Chief Reports," *Daily Press* (January 13, 1952).

[206] Ibid.

[207] "Special Fund to Pay for Ambulance," *Daily Press* (October 13, 1947).

SSSSS - Article announcing the new ambulance service for Phoebus and the Chesapeake District on March 12, 1948 - Left to right, Chief of Police Norman R. Turner; A.G. Mittlemaier; the Rev. L. Hesnan; Engineer George Shelby; First Assistant Foreman A.L. Foster; Chief A.A. Schmidt, Sr.; Foreman; Benjamin C. Tyler; Paul LaBarber; Herbert C. Luther; Gilbert W. Johnson; and Officer Stephen Galla (Daily Press).

TTTTT - Fire Department and Robert F. Snow, Jr. in October 23, 1949 (Daily Press).

The first crop of first aid instructors at the Phoebus Fire Department were Chief A.A. Schmidt, Foreman Benjamin C. Tyler, Engineer Robert F. Snow Jr., William E. Snow and fireman Herbert Luther, Phoebus police Norman Turner, Phoebus Police sergeant James Hartley and Stephen Galla.[208]

On November 10, 1949, the ambulance crew of the Phoebus Fire Department had a "first" when they stopped to extinguish a car fire without

---

[208] "13 Men Qualify As First Aid Instructors," *Daily Press* (November 16, 1947).

any fire-fighting equipment. Robert F. Snow, Jr. and Bill J. Odom were making a hospital run when they saw a fire break out in the "late model car" belonging to Dr. Robert H. Wright of Phoebus. It was reported that they used the "bucket brigade" method of olden days to extinguish the fire.[209] In January 1951 the Phoebus Fire Department bought a red-and-chrome 800-gallon fire engine from the Oren-Roanoke Company of Roanoke, Virginia for $12,300.[210] The Fire Department immediately painted the blue seal of the Town of Phoebus on the door.[211]

UUUUU - Mr. and Mrs. Tony Ingorgiola donate $1000 to the Phoebus Fire Department to partially fund the new fire truck. Chief Schmidt accepts on behalf of the fire department in 1950 (Daily Press).

---

[209] "Ambulance Men Put Out Blaze," *Daily Press* (November 10, 1949).
[210] "It Shines Like $12,300," *Daily Press* (January 14, 1951).
[211] "It's All Yours Mayor," *Daily Press* (January 14, 1951).

VVVVV - Engineers Charles L. Hill (left) and George L. Selby (right) put the finishing touches to the first shine on January 13, 1951 (Daily Press).

WWWWW - Engineer C. R. Bryant, (left) representative of the Oren-Roanoke Company accepts a check from Phoebus Mayor Leo J. Taylor on January 13, 1951 (Daily Press).

XXXXX - Phoebus First Aid Squad in 1953 (Martha Morris).

YYYYY - Photo for the 1953 Firemen's Convention in Phoebus (Martha Morris).

ZZZZZ - Poster from the 2008 Phoebus Days designed by Terrie Hale Viars (Nancy Blagg).

	Pride of Phoebus Spotlight **Anton Alexander Schmidt** Fire Chief for 30 years (1933-1963) Life: 1886-1963

Anton Alexander (A.A.) Schmidt was better known in the Phoebus community as Tony and he served as the Phoebus Fire Chief for more than 30 years. Schmidt was born in Phoebus on October 5, 1886 and he joined the Fire Department as a Lamp Boy in 1905.

He was promoted to second assistant foreman on May 14, 1912 and, two weeks later, became the first assistant foreman. In 1917 he was elected assistant chief. Schmidt briefly became Fire Chief in 1930 and became the Fire Chief for 30 years starting in 1933.

PREPARING FOR MEMORIAL DAY PROGRAM
Flower arrangements to be placed today on graves of deceased members of Phoebus Volunteer Fire Company are prepared Friday night by, left to right, Gary Smith, Robert Snow III, Chief A. A. Schmidt and A. A. Schmidt III. A complement of 30 firemen in dress uniform will distribute flowers to six cemeteries early this morning.

AAAAAA - Gary Smith, Robert Snow III, Chief Schmidt, and his son A.A. Schmidt III prepare flower arrangements to put on deceased members of the Phoebus Fire Company on May 30, 1959 (Daily Press).

Although Schmidt was born into a world with no electricity and no cars, he worked in the woodworking department of NASA and was helping to get American astronauts to the moon when he died in 1963. According to his grandson, Tony Schmidt, Chief Schmidt would always ride his bike and meet the men at the fire in Phoebus.

Anton A. Schmidt

Phoebus Fire Company lost its most dedicated member last Friday night—Anton Alexander (Tony) Schmidt. Death ended a remarkable span of volunteer service; this man gave most of his spare time to a highly important community agency over a period of 58 years, without a penny of remuneration.

He joined the old Phoebus Fire Department in 1905 as a lamp boy, at the age of 18. Born in the Town of Phoebus, he lived there all his life, seeing it merge into the City of Hampton. The firefighting unit became a company of the municipal department, but through decades of change and expansion, Tony Schmidt's interest in its activities never flagged.

He rose through the ranks of the volunteer unit and became chief in 1933, serving in that capacity until his death. It is impossible to calculate how much time he gave to his community—surely it must have run into the tens of thousands of hours.

Chief Schmidt was a highly skilled craftsman, and worked hard at his vocation over most of his life. Actually, he took on two jobs, for there was no task that was too small or two big for him to accept and carry out for the Fire Company.

It is hardly necessary to add that such dedicated men deserve the gratitude of their fellow-citizens. Chief Schmidt made an unestimably great contribution to his home community—nearly six decades of tireless, freely-given and selfless service.

BBBBBB - Obituary of Chief Schmidt on May 8, 1963 (Daily Press).

8 CONSOLIDATION WITH HAMPTON: 1952-1984

In June 1952, Hampton, Elizabeth City County, and Phoebus embarked on consolidation efforts, and voters in all three areas voted to merge and become the new City of Hampton. Phoebus voted 562 to 99 to consolidate with Hampton.[212]

Hampton's former police chief Lloyd H. Nicholson recalled the consolidation 30 years later in 1982 saying that the early days were a difficult adjustment. "It was rough in the beginning. We had our ups and downs, but we did alright." Former Hampton vice mayor William L. Woodmansee said it took a while to adjust to consolidation. "There are still vestiges of factions from these three localities, although this has mostly disappeared."[213]

For the Phoebus Fire Department, the biggest initial change would be to its name. Going forward it would be called the Phoebus Volunteer Fire Company, and the Phoebus Station was designated as Hampton Fire Department Station 2, because it was second oldest company in the city. Years later, the Hampton Division of Fire and Rescue adopted the Phoebus Fire Department motto "Citizen's First".[214]

In an interview for this book, Paul Sulzberger spoke of how, no matter what the name or year, the Phoebus Fire Department was always a family. Sulzberger joined the Fire Department the same year that Phoebus consolidated with Hampton (1952) and served for 67 years.

When Sulzberger wanted to marry his wife of 55 years from Panama, fellow fireman John Mugler helped him with the extraordinary amount of government paperwork. Later, Paul would suffer a fall from a roof and break his back in 1966. He said the entire community of Phoebus provided

---

[212] Dick Solito, "Phoebus, ECC and Hampton to Consolidate," *Daily Press* (June 18, 1982).

[213] Robert Graves, "Consolidated Hampton Turns 30 Today," *Daily Press* (July 1, 1982).

[214] "History of the Phoebus Volunteer Fire Department" *Phoebus Volunteer Fire Department* (2019), 3.

an extraordinary amount of assistance to him and his family. Sulzberger still feels very lucky that the fall only crushed his spine and didn't sever it. He still retained use of his legs and was able to walk with the use of braces and crutches and he was able to stay with the Fire Department as a statistician. "There are three things I love in this world, said Sulzberger, "My family, Phoebus, and God."

CCCCCC - Paul Sulzberger in 1964.

Sulzberger remembers the fire engines responding to fires and grabbing him and members of his family on the corner. When the call went out, merchants from Phoebus businesses would leave their store and run and jump on the firetruck as it rolled down Mellen Street, on its way to the fire. Maver Clarke, E.L. Clarke's wife, once claimed she was worried that Ernest would miss jumping on the truck and fall on his face!

Long-time fireman, and current chaplain for the Phoebus company, Don Blagg said the first engine would head to the fire, while the second engine would go around town and pick up the volunteers. Sometimes the stop would include a stop to Fuller's, the popular watering hole, to pick up the volunteers. "Doctors, lawyers, and shop owners would be excused for fires," said Blagg. Even Judge Carmel would stop his court proceedings and head off to fight a fire. Blagg said he remembered grabbing Judge Carmel and helping him onto the trucks in those days. "He was as light as a feather."

"At one time, all members were from Phoebus," said former Volunteer Fire Chief Henry "Hank" Beimler. He remembers tagging along with his own father and grandfather, who were both members. Beimler later joined the company at age 16 in 1969."[215]

For Sulzberger, fighting fires was also a family affair. Four members of his family were always heading to the same fires including himself, his father, and brothers. "The whole town would turn out to fight the fires. I remember that George Wilder would even sleep with his clothes on to get to the Fire Station faster," he said.

Sulzberger started working as a roofer at 9 years old and joined the Fire Department at 15 years old as the Phoebus Fire Department was consolidating with the city of Hampton. He remembers that in the early years at least, Phoebus kept its independence. "There were 125 volunteers in Phoebus. Phoebus and Charlottesville always had the largest companies."

During our conversation, Sulzberger reminisced about the boys that joined him in the early 1950s including Tommy Smith, Jerry Scharf, and Billy Hardin who were all kids when they joined the fire company.

Blagg said the fire company was a place where boys could go to stay out of

---

[215] Deborah Hyman, "A Firefighting Century in Phoebus" (*Daily Press*, July 29, 1993).

trouble by having mentors in the community and learning skills, along with playing pool. "We would be in charge of washing the fire truck and taking care of the German Shepherd named Lady."

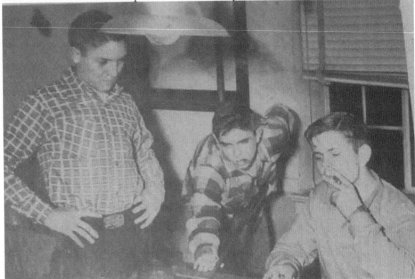

DDDDDD - Melvin Johnson, Tommy Smith and Paul Sulzberger playing pool at the fire station around 1953 (Paul Sulzberger).

EEEEEE - George Alsing, Melvin Johnson, Tommy Smith, and Paul Sulzberger playing cards at the fire station around 1953 (Paul Sulzberger).

FFFFFF - Apprentice Harry Mugler in 1963 (Daily Press).

Young recruits started out as apprentices when they were between 15-20 years old. In Phoebus they were called "latern boys" like the early days of

Chief Schmidt.[216] The latern boys needed their parents permission and needed to be recommended by someone at the Phoebus Fire Company to join. Over time they would ride on the trucks to fires and learn how to fight fires with seasoned veterans from the company. The Phoebus Fire Company had 17 latern boys in 1963 alone.[217]

Phoebus and the 1953 Firemen's Convention

Phoebus played host to the 1953 Virginia Firemen's Convention from August 9-14, 1953. It was expected to be the largest event in the history of the organization with approximately 2,000 delegates and their families attending from around the state.[218] Coming soon after consolidation, all of Hampton was "gaily bedecked with red, white, ad blue bunting for the five-day convention"[219]

Meeting jointly were the state fire chiefs, women's auxiliaries, and the firemen. Highlighting the week were a range of business, social, and competitive events. The 1953 convention also included a demonstration air-sea rescue, a clam bake, and street dance.[220]

The week-long convention began with the opening of the State Fire Chief's meeting at the Hotel Chamberlin on Monday, August 10, 1953. A. A. Schmidt, Sr., of Phoebus was the host for the kick-off event and was saluted for his nearly 50 years of volunteer fire fighting. Business meetings and panel discussions took place all day on August 10 with Lieutenant Governor A.E.S. Stephens delivering remarks at a banquet later that night.[221]

A memorial service for deceased members was conducted at 8 p.m. on Wednesday night at the Phoebus Methodist Church followed by street

---

[216] Betsy Edison, "When Fire Sire Sounds, Junior Volunteers Answer Alarm" (*Daily Press*, June 23, 1963).
[217] Ibid.
[218] "Social, Business Events Scheduled As Hampton Set to Welcome 2,000 Firemen," *Daily Press* (August 9, 1953).
[219] Ibid.
[220] "Firemen Begin Week-Long Conclave in Phoebus Area," *Daily Press* (August 10, 1953).
[221] Ibid.

dance at the Phoebus Recreation Center from 9 p.m. until midnight.[222] In a bit of irony, J. E. Jeffers of the Esso Standard Oil Company in Newport News came to the convention to demonstrate how to control a large fire control. As we will see later, Esso might have needed more practice.

GGGGGG - The Phoebus Fire Company is bedecked with bunting and welcome signs for the State Firemen's Convention on August 9, 1953 (Phoebus Fire Company).

There were lots of fun programs on Thursday, August 13 beginning with a first aid contest at 8:30 a.m., followed by a four-man hose contest at 11 a.m., a one-man hose coupling contest at 1 p.m., a motor and chemical contest at 1:30 p.m., a four-man ladder contest at 3 p.m., a six-man ladder contest took place at 4 p.m., and it was followed by a 100-yard foot race at 5 p.m. There was also a mock water battle between a "team of Mountaineers" and the Phoebus Company that afternoon.[223]

Thursday's events ended with a band concert by the Peninsula Community Band and the grand ball and coronation of Jacqueline G. Bates as "Miss Flame." The week culminated with a large parade through the business district of Phoebus on Mellen and Mallory on the morning of Friday, August 14.[224] The parade began on Buckroe Highway at Rosevale and marched to Mellen Street down to Willard Avenue to the Phoebus playground where refreshments were served. There were 2000 men and

---

[222] "Social, Business Events Scheduled As Hampton Set to Welcome 2,000 Firemen," *Daily Press* (August 9, 1953).
[223] Ibid.
[224] Ibid.

women in marching units and 100 pieces of fire equipment.

The Phoebus Fire Company also attempted to break a record for Peninsula blood donations by collecting 400 pints of blood. Among the initial volunteers for the bloodmobile visit were 25 men from the Naval Ordnance Laboratory and 36 men from the USS Stallion, a Navy mine layer.[225] They unfortunately fell short of the record.[226]

HHHHHH - Officers of the Phoebus Volunteer Fire Department in this 1953. Seated, left to right: A.A. Schmidt, Chief; W.L. Selby, Sr., assistant chief; and R.F. Snow, Jr. fireman; Standing, left to right: A.L. Foster, first assistant fireman; C.H. Warren, treasurer; E.J. Sulzberger, president; T.H. Fetters, statistician; and C.U. Stowell, corresponding secretary. Other officers not in this photo were E.L. Hale, secretary and R.D. Selby, second assistant foreman.

---

[225] "Firemen Begin Week-Long Conclave in Phoebus Area," *Daily Press* (August 10, 1953).
[226] Ibid.

FIREMEN'S CONVENTION COMMITTEE MAKES FINAL PLANS

IIIIII – The Phoebus Fire Company going over the book for the 1953 convention. Left to right are A. G. Mittlemaier, John P. Mugler, Robert F. Snow Jr., C. F. Patton and Chief A.A. Schmidt on August 10, 1953 (Daily Press).

JJJJJJ - Mellen Street in Phoebus in the 1950s (Martha Morris).

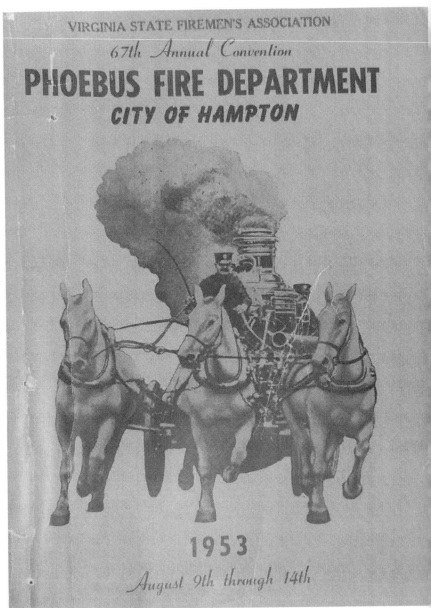

KKKKKK - Program for the Virginia State Firemen's Association's 67th Annual Convention in Phoebus on August 9-14, 1953. (Martha Morris).

In recounting all of the fires of the past, Paul Sulzberger pointed out the fire at the Esso Standard Oil Terminal in Newport News, a massive fire that is generally forgotten today.

LLLLLL - Fire at the Esso Bunker Oil Station in Newport News. April 1958 (Daily Press).

In April 1958 hundreds of civilian and military firefighters battled for 39 hours to extinguish the fire at Esso Standard Oil Terminal at the Newport News Boat Harbor. Daily Press photographers were on hand to capture what, at the time, was the largest and most costly fire in lower Peninsula history.[227] Sulzberger said that Phoebus firefighters were on staff for 72 hours during that fire. The Daily Press reported on April 25, 1958, that Phoebus firefighter Monroe Goodrich of 15 Sewell Avenue suffered some of the most serious injuries. He was treated at Dixie Hospital and was later reported in good condition.[228]

---

[227] "Look back: Esso Standard Oil Company Fire," *Daily Press* (April 15, 2018).
[228] "Entire Tank Farm May Be Doomed," *Daily Press* (April 25, 1958).

MMMMMM - Fire at the Esso Bunker Oil Station in Newport News. April 1958 (Daily Press).

NNNNNN - Hampton Fire Marshall Frank F. Hopkins accepts delivery of a new $19,000 pumper in June 1959. Robert J. Smith is a driver of the Phoebus Company where the fire engine has been assigned (Daily Press).

OOOOOO - New Officers of the Phoebus Fire Company on February 14, 1960. Left to right, front row, Macy M. Carmel, president; Ray Wilt, secretary; Jack Wilkerson, corresponding secretary; Nelson Fuller, treasurer; E.J. Sulzberger, chaplain; and Preston Conroy, statistician; and back row A.A. Schmidt, Chief; Alford I. Foster, deputy chief; Robert F. Snow, Jr., first assistant chief; M.J. Goodrich, second assistant chief; and Raymond D. Selby, captain. (Daily Press).

The 1963 Firemen's Convention book gives many details on the Phoebus Fire Company that year. "At the present time the company has 69 active members, 5 honorary members, and 13 junior firemen; 4 of the junior firemen are now in the Armed Forces. The fire schools are sponsored by the City of Hampton and each company has its own fire drills. The voluntary service of these men saves thousands of tax dollars that would have to be paid were it not for their unselfish efforts. It has been said that no organization contributes more to the community than does a Fire Company or Department.

The officers of the Phoebus Company for the year of 1963 were Chief Robert F. Snow, Jr., Deputy Chief Gilbert Johnson, First Assistant Chief R.D. Selby, 2nd Assistant Chief Clyde Norman, Captain John Tyler,

President Macy Carmel, Vice President Jack Wilkerson, Recording Secretary W.H. Griffin, Corresponding Secretary George Anderson, Treasurer Nelson Fuller, Statistician P.T. Conroy, and Chaplain Emil Sulzberger. Nelson.

1963 would also mark the end of an era with the passing of Chief Schmidt who led the Phoebus Fire Department for more than 30 years. In the photo taken before the 1963 Virginia State Firefighter's Association convention, there is an empty chair to mark the absence left by Chief Schmidt.

PPPPPP - 1963 Firemen's Convention Bottom row, left to right: T. Craigs, E.L. Kaiser, H. Luther, J.P. Mugler, G. Anderson, W. Griffin, P.R. Wilt, M. Carmel, Vacant Chair for Chief Schmidt who passed away that year, G.W. Johnson, R.F. Snow, Jr. R.D. Selby, C.D. Norman, C.G. Mugler, A.G. Mittlemaier, A.H. Mittlemaier, A.I. Foster, and M. Wells. Second row, left to right: C. Klein, G.W. Selby, H. Mugler, C. Lina, F. Woolridge, A.G. Mittlemaier, Jr. M.J. Goodrich, D. Purnell, J. Wilkerson, T. Mugler, J. Craig, M.E. Alligood, R.E. Mingee, D. Thompson, R. Smith, T.D. Smith, W.I. Smith, B. Purnell, A.A. Schmidt III, S. Galla, C.H. Warren, Jr., C. Patton, J.D. Smith, D. Norman, C.A. Hellman, Sr., D. Jordan, V. Hellman, B. Deweese, T. Monta, C. Stowell, D. Purnell, Wm. Selby, G. Wilder, G. Smith, T. Craig, R. Edwards, L.P. Sulzberger, Sr., R. Parker, J. Tyler, H. Biemler, R.F. Snow III, S. Harrison, P. Sulzberger. (Tony Schmidt).

QQQQQQ – *Officers of the Phoebus Fire Company during the 1963 Virginia's Firemen's Association convention in Hampton. Left to right: George Anderson, Corresponding Secretary; P.R. Wilt, Captain; Macy Carmel, President; G.W. Johnson, Deputy Chief; R.D. Selby, 1st Assistant Chief; Clyde D. Norman, 2nd Assistant Chief; C.G. Mugler, Acting Chaplain. Absent from picture: Nelson Fuller, Treasurer; J. Wilkinson, Vice-President; P.T. Conroy, Statistician; E.J. Sulzberger, Chaplain. (Amy Lee Smith).*

RRRRRR - *Phoebus Fire Company captures first place in the four-man ladder team at the Virginia Firemen's Convention in the 1960s. Members were Joe Sanzo, Blackstone Purnell, Tommy Smith, and George Wilder (Pam Sanzo).*

SSSSSS - Phoebus Fire Company installed officers on February 22, 1964 at the Chateau Restaurant. Phoebus Volunteer Fire Company officer, from left to right, Ray Mingee, secretary; Gil Johnson, chief; John Tyler, deputy chief; Emil Sulzberger, chaplain; Boots Selby, first assistant; Macy Carmel, president; Clyde Norman, second assistant; and George Wilder, captain (Daily Press).

TTTTTT - New administrative officer for the Phoebus Fire Company on February 17, 1967. New administrative officers for the Phoebus Volunteer Fire Company in 1967 are, from left to right, F.J. Woolridge, vice president; Raymond E. Mingee, recording secretary; Thomas A. Mugler, corresponding secretary; M.J. Goodrich, statistician; Walter H. Saunders, treasurer; and Robert L. Blagg, chaplain (Daily Press).

UUUUUU - The Phoebus Fire Company receives the first diesel-powered fire truck on the Peninsula, a 1,000-gallon pumper in 1968 (Hampton City: Fire Dept).

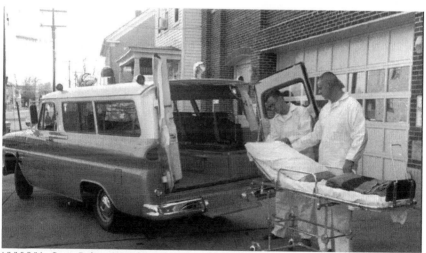

VVVVVV - Capt. Robert W. Edwards and Lt. Paul Sulzberger inspect the new ambulance for the Phoebus Fire Company's Volunteer Rescue Unit in April 1964. The 1964 ambulance was a converted station wagon and cost $3,800. For the first time, it carried a new type of stretcher that could be extended to hospital bed height. (Hampton City: Fire Dept. - Equipment).

WWWWWW - Phoebus Fire Company in 1963 (Paul Sulzberger).

XXXXXX - Ernest L. "Bubba" Hale as a dispatcher in the 1960s (Pam Hale Johnson).

77th ANNUAL VIRGINIA STATE FIREMEN'S CONVENTION
CONVENTION COMMITTEES

ENTERTAINMENT COMMITTEE

Nelson Fuller, Chairman
Preston T. Conroy, Co-Chairman
Bernard D. Stimson
Anton A. Schmidt, III
Richard Purnell
Gary Smith

Clyde Lina
Paul Sulzberger
Richard C. Norman
Clyde Norman
John Tyler
Gilbert W. Johnson

Harold Carpenter
Victor Hellman
J. Thomas Craigs
George Anderson
Jack Wilkinson
Don DeBlasio

MUSIC COMMITTEE

William H. Griffin, Jr., Chairman
John Tyler
Andrew H. Mittelmaier
Stephen Galla

Robert Miller
Alfred Bohn
Joseph L. Craigs
Walter Furneyhough

Earnest Hale
Robert F. Snow, Jr.

CONVENTION PROGRAM COMMITTEE

Preston T. Conroy, Chairman
Charles Stowell

Wallace Hicks
John P. Mugler

C. Guy Mugler
Edward Smith

HEADQUARTERS AND REGISTRATION COMMITTEE

Raymond Mingee, Jr., Chairman
Robert Miller
Thomas Monta

David Young
William L. Smith
Daniel Jordan

Carl Hellman, III
Leonard Sulzberger
Wayne Harding

RECEPTION COMMITTEE

B. Mack Wells, Chairman
Thomas D. Smith
Robert J. Smith

C. Allan Eacho
Sherman Ford
Hugh Loughran

L. Edgar Mingee, Sr.

PRIZES, RULES AND CONTEST COMMITTEE

Albert G. Mittelmaier, Chairman
B. Mack Wells, Co-Chairman
Charles Stowell
Sidney Klein
Thomas Mugler
Anton Schmidt, III

Richard Purnell
Thomas D. Smith
Clyde Lina
George Wilder
Blackstone Purnell
Charles Sanso

Charles A. Schmidt
Gilbert W. Johnson
Thomas Monta
Nelson Harrison
Wayne Harding

PUBLICITY COMMITTEE

Nelson Fuller, Chairman
Andrew Greenwell, Daily Press
Wallace Hicks

Wilton Schmidt
Dick Kidney, WGH
Ben C. Tyler

Robert F. Snow, Jr.

PROGRAM BOOKLET COMMITTEE

Macy M. Carmel, Chairman
John P. Mittelmaier
Leonard C. Pierce

Raymond D. Selby
Edward F. Ware
Charles Warren, Jr.

Charles Patton
Fred Ellis Enterprises
Robert F. Snow, Jr.

DECORATIONS COMMITTEE

Raymond D. Selby, Chairman
M. Carmel, Co-Chairman
William L. Smith
Robert F. Snow, III
Gary Smith
George Selby, Jr.

Thomas Mugler
Clyde Lina
Harold Carpenter
Paul Sulzberger
Fred J. Wooldridge, Sr.
Lewis Sulzberger, Sr.

William DeWeese
Wilford Hale
Nelson Harrison
Thomas Monta
Daniel Jordan

FIRST AID COMMITTEE

Robert Edwards, Chairman
Charles Stowell
Richard Purnell
Paul Sulzberger

Herbert Luther
William E. Snow
Douglas Smith
Dr. O. W. Ward, Sr.

Dr. Oscar W. Ward, Jr.
Dr. F. A. Kearney
Monroe J. Goodrich

PARADE COMMITTEE

Macy Carmel, Chairman
Raymond D. Selby, Co-Chairman
George L. Selby, Sr.
Richard Purnell
Preston T. Conroy
Anton A. Schmidt, III

Gary Smith
Paul Sulzberger
Judge Frank A. Kearney
Andrew G. Mittelmaier
Perry Carmel
Lewis P. Sulzberger, Sr.

Charles Biefeldt
Thomas H. Fetters, Sr.
Ernest L. Clark
Alford L. Foster
Wray R. Lancer
Jack Wilkinson

FINANCE COMMITTEE

John P. Mugler, Chairman
Emil Sulzberger

David J. Zephier
Morris S. Cooper

Isadore A. Saunders

MEMORIAL COMMITTEE

Emil Sulzberger, Chairman
C. Guy Mugler, Co-Chairman
John Kaiser

J. Thomas Craigs
Robert S. Miller
Carl Hellman, Jr.

William Kyle
Alford L. Foster

HOUSING COMMITTEE

Frank J. Welch, Chairman
Mrs. Grace Alligood, Co-Chairman
Malcolm Alligood
Robert Edwards

Daniel Jordan
Jack Wilkinson
Thomas F. Gibbons
Leonard M. Newcombe

Buckroe: Milton Ghivizzani
Wythe: J. E. Wilson

FIRE HOUSE COMMITTEE

Thomas H. Fetters, Sr., Chairman
Sidney Klein
B. Mack Wells
Robert Smith

Paul Sulzberger
William L. Selby, Sr.
Leo Sulzberger
Douglas Smith

John R. Kaiser
Emil J. Schmidt, Jr.
Wilton E. Schmidt
Henry A. Schmidt, Jr.

YYYYYY - 1963 State Firemen's Convention Committees for the Phoebus Fire Company (Tom Jackson).

ZZZZZ - The Phoebus Fire Company Rescue Squad in 1963. Front row, left to right: M. Wells, W. Griffin, M. Alligood, L.P. Sulzberger, Captain R. Edwards, C. Stowell, T. Mugler, J.P. Mugler, D. Purnell, B. Purnell. Second row, left to right: R.D. Selby, J. Tyler, M. Carmel, A.L. Foster, J. Wilkerson, W.I. Smith, A.H. Mittlemaier, D. Smith, R.F. Snow, Jr., M.J. Goodrich, P. Sulzberger, G. Smith, T. Smith, G.W. Selby, Jr., G. Wilder, C. Norman. Third row, left to right: A.A. Schmidt, III, R. Smith, P.R. Wilt, C. Lina, S. Klein, G.W. Johnson.

Professional Firefighting vs. Volunteers

As the 20th century progressed alongside the firefighting skills and technology there became a need for full-time professional firefighting at the Phoebus Fire Company and to examine the overall command structure.

After consolidation with Hampton in 1952, the city started adding professional, paid firemen into each fire company in the city. Acting City Manager for Hampton C.E. Johnson addressed this move in 1954.

"At the present time, Hampton has a paid fire department staff of 21 men, including the fire marshal and two dispatchers. In three of the five fire stations, there are only two men on duty at a time, and in the other two stations, only one man on duty per shift This means that when an alarm is sounded, the fire apparatus responds with only one man, the driver aboard. When it arrives, the apparatus must await volunteer firemen before it can be put in operation. Now we will agree that there are times when volunteer firemen happen to be in the station when an alarm sounds and therefore they can go out with the apparatus. Also, we will agree that there are times when volunteer firemen arrive before the apparatus. Even so, these instances in the past do not constitute a guarantee in the future."[229]

---

[229] "Full-Time Firemen and Insurance Rates," *Daily Press* (December 13, 1954).

"It is not to be denied that Hampton is highly dependent upon its volunteer fire companies, which have carried the burden of fighting Hampton's fires for many years. But, as officials have pointed out in a previous report, Hampton's situation today is such that volunteer companies cannot be made the sole protection of life and property. The city is too large and a more modern means of fire-fighting must be adopted sooner or later."[230] The numbers of paid firefighters would continue to grow over the years as would tensions with volunteers.

In 1963 paid firefighters worked a 24-hour shift every other day, drove the trucks and generally worked alongside with the volunteers in polishing the trucks and floors and taking care of other equipment.[231]

By 1975 Hampton would be taking a hard look at how to structure the city's dual paid-volunteer fire companies. Should volunteer or paid firemen command Hampton firefighters at the fire scene? What should be the correct mix of paid and volunteer firefighters?[232]

The command structure in 1975 for most fire companies in Hampton had been unchanged since consolidation with Hampton in 1952. That structure placed the fire marshal at the top, followed by five levels of volunteer officers before paid firemen.

"I don't think you can run a modern department of this size efficiently with that type of command structure," said Frank A. Kearney III, a familiar name in this book and president of the Hampton Professional Firemen's Association (HPFA) at that time. He thought the command structure was outdated and inefficient and he advocated for placing paid firemen nearer the top of the fire companies. Kearney said that command structure was worked out during consolidation when one department was formed from several separate fire departments, adding that the antiquated system was confusing and potentially dangerous. "We believe it's time the chain of command be changed in the city of Hampton to place the professional firemen in charge at the scene of fires instead of the volunteer firemen. Right now a professional captain at a fire is under the command of a

---

[230] "Full-Time Firemen and Insurance Rates," *Daily Press* (December 13, 1954).
[231] Betsy Edison, "When Fire Sire Sounds, Junior Volunteers Answer Alarm" (*Daily Press*, June 23, 1963).
[232] Al Christopher, "Fire Department Organization Given Close Scrutiny" (*Daily Press*, November 8, 1975).

volunteer captain. In a big fire there's no coordination. Each department is doing its own thing. Everybody should know what his job is and go do it," said Kearney.[233]

J. R. Edwards, then chief of Northampton Volunteer Fire Company, disagreed with Kearney's assessment. "The reason volunteer officers are often in command positions is because many have as much firefighting experience or more than many paid firemen." For instance, in 1975 Ralph Ghivizzani, chief of Buckroe Beach Volunteer Fire Company, had 18 years' experience, had the shortest service of the city's six volunteer chiefs. Edwards believed that the command procedures had proved adequate. "If you had a paid department with the firefighting experience and schooled in firefighting then I'd say 'yes, the volunteers should be under them,' but that's not the case. Some paid men don't have as much experience as the volunteers," said Edwards.[234]

City officials had to make tough decisions on what approach that thought would be most effective. This issue would cause feuds for years to come. The issue would get worse before it got better. An article in 1977 put a spotlight on the sparring between volunteer and paid firemen in the region.

"In Hampton, paid firefighters say the volunteers aren't dependable and join the force mainly to socialize. In York County, rescue squad patients are taken to the hospital by way of the fire station, so paid fire and rescue workers can get off the ambulance and volunteers can get on to make the rest of the trip. At the root of the problem in these communities are a lack of manpower and disagreement over the role of volunteers. Volunteer firemen outnumber paid fire staffs in the six communities that make up the Peninsula's 310,000 population - but professional firefighters claim they do most of the work. The volunteers, with beginnings steeped in community tradition, are showing signs of resistance against what they fear is professional takeover."[235]

Everything was met with a challenge from both sides, even the color of the fire trucks. Frank Kearney III chastised Hampton for not hiring enough firefighters to furnish adequate protection. In most cases, Kearney said, only one or two paid personnel per engine and there was no guarantee that

---

[233] Al Christopher, "Fire Department Organization Given Close Scrutiny" (*Daily Press*, November 8, 1975).
[234] Ibid.
[235] "Volunteer and Paid Firemen Feuding," *The Danville Register* (October 13, 1977).

the city's 450 volunteers would show up at a fire. "We might drive up to a fire with only two men and engines and that's pretty embarrassing," Kearney explained.[236]

Volunteers in Hampton outnumbered professional firefighters nearly 3 to 1 in 1977, and some volunteers had more rank than fighters who spend all their time on the job. Kearney believed professionals should oversee volunteers because they have more training.[237]

Tensions would continue throughout the 1980s as Hampton would try to fix the situation by a variety of means including establishing a formal training academy to work to increase company proficiency and cohesion between the paid and volunteer firefighters.[238]

Hampton Battalion Chief Sidney Klein acknowledged in 1980 that actions on the fire line showed "serious deficiencies in the way we do things." Klein said that paid and volunteers tend to "go off in different directions at a fire and that this training program was intended to remedy that situation."[239]

Volunteers battle fire chief's plans
After 2 years, firefighters continue to lack cohesion

AAAAAAA - Headline from June 1989 (Daily Press).

---

[236] "Volunteer and Paid Firemen Feuding," *The Danville Register* (October 13, 1977).
[237] Ibid.
[238] David Chernicky, "Hampton Fire Training Program Becoming a Hot Potato" (*Daily Press*, November 20, 1980).
[239] Ibid.

BBBBBBB - Frank Maida (right) of Phoebus Rescue Squad gets checks totaling $2,400, for the cardiac fund, while H. Warren Landis, Donna Norvell and Harold Simmons looks on in 1979 (Hampton City: Fire Dept. - Personnel).

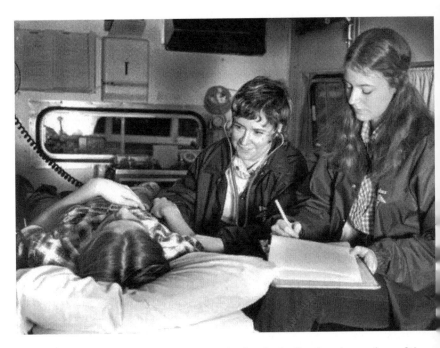

CCCCCCC - 1976/ Sandy Maglin (left) and Vicki Church, the first female members of the Phoebus volunteer rescue squad, administer to a patient. (Hampton City: Fire Dept. - Equipment).

Pride of Phoebus Spotlight
Clyde Joseph Norman
Fire Chief
Phoebus Restaurant Owner 1951-1998
Life: 1924-2014

Clyde Norman came to Phoebus in 1949 to visit his sister and never left. Norman would be actively involved in the community affairs of Phoebus serving as president of the Phoebus Civic Association, a member of the City of Hampton Planning Commission and the Chief and life member of Phoebus Volunteer Fire Company.

Today Norman is remembered fondly for his restaurants. Norman opened his first business, the Virginia Cafe, in 1951 on Mallory Street. He moved the restaurant to the Buckroe area in 1958 and re-christened it the U.S. Grill. He opened Clyde's Restaurant on Mallory Street in 1962 and moved it to 28 East Mellen Street in 1986.

Clyde was a veteran of WWII and honored as the Grand Marshall of the 1991 Phoebus Days Parade. "I think it's really great that people have that kind of respect for me," says Norman. "I've tried to do my part for the community, to be good to people and to earn their respect. I am very honored."

DDDDDDD - Nelson Fuller and Clyde Norman in the 1980s (Amy Lee Smith).

9 ROSELAND FIRE:
1985

One of the biggest fires in Phoebus history destroyed the home of its namesake, Harrison Phoebus. The home had many names through the years including Roseland, Roseland Manor, the Strawberry Banks Manor House, and simply the Manor House. It was built on the property once occupied by Joseph Segar's Roseland Farm and for nearly a century the Gilded Age mansion stood as a community landmark until it was destroyed by fire on an early March morning in 1985.

In 1978 the Virginia Historic Landmarks Commission declared it a state landmark because of its architectural style and it would later be on the National Register of Historic Places. The Châteauesque Queen Anne-style mansion was designed by a New York architect Arthur Crooks and was extremely rare for Virginia. This type of house was more common in places like New York and Newport, Rhode Island at the end of the 19th century.[240]

EEEEEEE - Roseland Manor in 1900 (Hampton Public Library).

---

[240] Lynda R. Page, "Manor house gutted," *Daily Press* (April 1, 1985).

There were reports that Roseland Manor was started by the New York Yacht Club in the 1880s and that organization chose the site on the Hampton Roads shore for a Southern terminal, [241] but abandoned those efforts. After going through property records at the Hampton Circuit Court we found these reports to be fictional. Harrison and his wife Annie Phoebus bought most of the Roseland Manor estate property from Caleb C. Willard and his wife Lucy on October 18, 1884. Harrison would have the house built during 1885 and into 1886. Much like his work on the opulent Hygeia Hotel, Phoebus added many luxuries for its day including indoor water.[242]

Sadly, Harrison Phoebus would die of a heart attack on February 25, 1886 at the age of 45 and he never got to see his home completed. His wife Annie and her seven children moved in around August 1887 and lived there until her death in 1906. After the death of Annie Phoebus, the executors of the estate were unable to find a buyer until 1919 when New York raincoat manufacturer Clarence Kenyon purchased Roseland Manor and its approximately 50 acres for his wife Mamie for $125,000.[243]

To prepare the estate for entertaining for her New York friends, Mrs. Kenyon added bathrooms, European artwork, high back wicker chairs, and crystal chandeliers. She also imported exotic trees and shrubberies for her formal garden. When Mr. Kenyon died in 1956, Mrs. Kenyon sold the house to William Ferguson Jr., owner of Strawberry Banks Motel. Ferguson would buy the property in 1957 and let Mrs. Kenyon live there for three more years until her death in 1960.[244]

The property ran a summer-dinner theatre in the 1960s and was used for parties, receptions, and even weddings over the years. The first two floors would later be turned into an office building around 1980. The high ceilings, wood floors, and brick exterior were reworked to make it suitable for offices at a cost of $100,000 at the time.[245]

---

[241] Lynda R. Page, "Manor house gutted," *Daily Press* (April 1, 1985).
[242] Ibid.
[243] "Mrs. Kenyon Buys Roseland, Paying $125,000 for It," *Daily Press* (July 22, 1919).
[244] Lynda R. Page, "Manor house gutted," *Daily Press* (April 1, 1985).
[245] Ibid.

The Roseland Fire

The fire began around 2:30 a.m. on Sunday, March 31, 1985. Five fire engines and two ladder trucks responded to the fire call at 10 Strawberry Banks Lane. Ten hours and 720,000 gallons of water later, only a few blackened chimneys and scorched walls remained.[246]

By 11 a.m., the Daily Press reported that "firefighters quietly watched clouds of smoke pour from a window of the once-grand 19th-century mansion. A few remaining flames played along the windowsill. The lawn, once a showplace for lavish entertaining, now consisted of miniature rivers flowing around mud-banks."[247]

Don Blagg was on the scene that night and morning. "It burned all night and we could see the flames from Curry Street and it burned all night long," he said. Blagg remembers seeing Roseland still smoldering and the grounds completely underwater the next morning."

Manor house gutted

99-year-old landmark to be razed

By LYNDA R. PAGE
Staff Writer

HAMPTON — An blaze early Sunday morning transformed the historic Strawberry Banks Manor House — formerly Roseland Manor — into a charred skeleton.

Five fire engines and two ladder trucks responded to the 2:30 a.m. fire call at 10 Strawberry Banks Lane. Ten hours and 720,000 gallons of water later, only a few blackened chimneys and scorched walls remained.

Officials said no one was in the building when the fire began. The cause of the fire is unknown.

At 11 a.m., firefighters quietly watched clouds of smoke pour from a window of the once-grand 19th-century mansion, which had been turned into

Hampton firefighters used 720,000 gallons of water to put out the blaze, whose cause was unknown.

FFFFFFF - Headline on April 1, 1985 (Daily Press).

Firefighters and equipment remained at the scene until 3:30 p.m. and security guards kept watch on property for days to keep sightseers away

---

[246] Lynda R. Page, "Manor house gutted," *Daily Press* (April 1, 1985).
[247] Ibid.

who arrived to see a beloved community treasure destroyed, much like the crowds that arrived 65 years before at the fire of the first Chamberlin Hotel.[248] Fire transformed the historic home into a "charred skeleton" on March 31 and it was so severely damaged that fire officials never determined the fire's cause.[249]

In an interview in July 1985, Carl Wallace, Hampton's fire marshal, said the smoke and fire detection system telephoned a hotel on the property three times to alert someone of the fire. The calls "apparently were not appropriately received," he said, declining to comment further.[250]

Phoebus would forever lose a major link to its past in 1985. Here are some photos of that iconic landmark:

GGGGGGG - Roseland Manor sitting next to the new Interstate 64 in 1957 (Tony Schmidt).

---

[248] Lynda R. Page, "Manor house gutted," *Daily Press* (April 1, 1985).
[249] "Roseland Manor," *Daily Press* (December 29, 1985).
[250] "Fire Alarms Protect Historic Sites," *Daily Press* (July 25, 1985).

HHHHHHH - Roseland Manor in 1963 (Daily Press).

IIIIIII - Roseland Manor in 1963 (Daily Press).

JJJJJJJ - Roseland Manor in 1977 (Daily Press).

KKKKKKK - John Banks was the caretaker of Roseland Manor in 1977 (Daily Press).

LLLLLLL - Roseland Manor in 1985 (Daily Press).

MMMMMMM - Phoebus Firefighter on the scene on March 31, 1985 (Daily Press).

NNNNNNN - Roseland Manor in 1985 (Daily Press).

OOOOOOO - The wrecking ball at Roseland Manor in 1985 (Daily Press).

PPPPPPP - Roseland Manor demolition in 1985 (Daily Press).

10 TODAY'S FIRE COMPANY: 1985-2019

The story of the past 30 years is the story that many have seen time and again in Phoebus. It's a tale of decline and rebuilding, of renovations and cutbacks and a resurgence.

100 Years of The Phoebus Hook and Ladder Company No. 1

Phoebus was once again chosen to host the Virginia State Firemen's Association's annual convention. The 107th version of the convention took place in 1993 and coincided with the 100th anniversary of the founding of the Phoebus Fire Department.[251]

QQQQQQQ - Phoebus Fire Company celebrating its 100th anniversary in 1993 (Phoebus Fire Company).

The event was a moment to stop and reflect on how volunteer firefighters had played a role in communities across Virginia. Events included a kickoff at the Chamberlin Hotel. "A parade, firefighter contests and exhibits are all a part of the free activities open to the public. The firefighters always look forward to the contests, where they can demonstrate their extensive training in the race against time - dressing, laying and connecting hoses, setting up and climbing ladders, and dropping supply lines off moving engines."[252]

To celebrate the anniversary, the Daily Press interviewed several firemen at

---

[251] Deborah Hyman, "A Firefighting Century in Phoebus," *Daily Press* (July 29, 1993).
[252] Ibid.

the Phoebus Fire Company to capture their stories about the current state of firefighting and how it had changed through the years.

"There was no breathing equipment or protective clothing. We wore street clothes and fought the fires until we couldn't stand the smoke. Even then, you would just get some fresh air, vomit, then go back," said William Griffin Jr. "I remember the old steamer that was pulled by horses. Like steam engines, it built up pressure and forced the water out. Kind of like what the modern engines do now," said George Selby, who joined the fire department in 1936.[253]

RRRRRRR - Longtime Phoebus Volunteer Fire Company member George Selby Sr., left, enjoys praise from Mayor James Eason and Margaret Schmitt, Hampton Volunteer Services at City Hall in May 1990. Selby, who was honored for 55 years of continuous service to the fire department (Daily Press).

It was a rite of passage for the Selby family. Selby's father, William, and two brothers Raymond and William, Jr. were also members in the early days.

---

[253] Deborah Hyman, "A Firefighting Century in Phoebus," *Daily Press* (July 29, 1993).

Even his granddaughter, Peggy Ross Boullianne, joined the fire department. Peggy became the first female firefighter in the company when she joined in 1980. "It's not the thrill, but the job that you do," said Selby. "You help your neighbor. It's really a good feeling being a fireman."[254]

The Phoebus Fire Company in 1993 included:

Members: A.G. Mittelmaier; H.C. Beimler, Jr., Chief; J.R. Collins, Captain; E. Snapp; G.I. Selby, Sr., President; F. Schaffer; P. Sulzberger; S. Galla, Chaplain; J.H. Wilkinson; R.E. Mingee, Junior Vice President; J.F. Wooldridge; M.E. Alligood; T. Kiser; R.D. Selby; K.C. Evans, Deputy Chief; C.M. Barkley; D. Heemstra; W.H. Griffin, Jr., Fire Assistant Chief; J.M. Adamowski, recording secretary; J.A. Barnett, secretary; S. Sanzo, Lieutenant; P.D. Seifert, statistician; S. Freel; F. Leviner; W.E. Selby; D.J. Galyon; B. Sanzo; C.W. Smith; AW. Hunt Jr.; J. Sanzo.

Life members: G.L. Selby Jr., second assistant chief; E.L. Hale, Treasurer; H.E. Carpenter; G.V. Hellman Sr.; W.T. Schmidt; L. Sulzberger; M. Wells; N.T. Fuller; CD. Norman; R.H. Smith; J.B. Tyler Jr.; D. Zephir; F.K. Gibbons; B.F. Purnell; W.E. Snow; O.W. Ward, Jr.

Trainees: J.R. Await; M. Dykas; H. Jaffe; L. Knight; M. King; D. Arron; S. Trenzado; H. Izum.

Continuing Rift

We've seen the rifts that occurred between career and volunteer firefighters back to 1954 when Hampton hired paid firefighters and brought them into an environment dominated at the time by volunteers. These issues would still be ongoing at the end of the 20th century. In 1989 Hampton had 240 full-time professional firefighters and more than 300 full-time volunteers.[255]

Hampton had brought in David T. McCarty from Colorado to be the city's Fire Chief in 1987. McCarty was recognized as an "excellent communicator and diplomat" and he was brought to Hampton to try "to bring together the paid staff and volunteers in an agreed set of procedures."[256]

[254254] Deborah Hyman, "A Firefighting Century in Phoebus," *Daily Press* (July 29, 1993).

[255] David Chernicky, "Volunteers Battle Fire Chief's Plans," *Daily Press* (June 5, 1989).

[256] Ibid.

An article in 1989 captured the ongoing tensions with some of the ways that McCarty was trying to move the Hampton Fire Department forward.

"While the paid, fire and rescue workers in the city give him high marks, volunteers have chastised him for what they see as a variety of failures. Contrary to the praise given by the colleague from McCarty's previous job in Colorado, one volunteer chief accuses him of not communicating with the volunteers and treating them unfairly. Friction between the career and volunteer firefighters is nothing new. The two sides have been bickering over authority, policy, and procedures since 1954."[257]

Lee Moore, chief of the Wythe volunteers, was one of McCarty's most vocal critics. "We've been totally ignored. Everything the volunteer chiefs have asked for has fallen on deaf ears," Moore said. He said the volunteer companies were afraid McCarty was trying to "erode their power by slowly reducing a volunteer officer's responsibility at the scene of fires and other emergencies."

"I think part of the resistance is because this department is very traditional. Very few changes have been made over the years," McCarty said. McCarty also countered complaints that he wasn't doing enough to recruit volunteers by launching a city-wide initiative to do just that. "If we're going to stick to a strategic plan and are serious about using the volunteers, let's get serious and have a citywide campaign with a full-time person behind it."

Lt. Jim Cross. President of the Hampton Professional Firefighters Association discussed McCarty's efforts. "I think he has made a good effort to bring harmony between the career and volunteers. The steps he has taken needed to be taken in order to have a progressive fire division," said Cross. "I think we'll continue as a combination department, not very much different than we are today," Cross said. "Without the volunteers, we would be operating a barebones fire department and certainly the level of fire service would not be as high."[258]

---

[257] David Chernicky, "Volunteers Battle Fire Chief's Plans," *Daily Press* (June 5, 1989).
[258] Ibid.

SSSSSS - Advertisement for volunteer firefighters on October 9, 1986 (Daily Press).

TTTTTTT - Hampton Fire and Rescue Services personnel in February 1990: back row, left to right: Robin Brock, volunteer secretary, fire investigations; David Coleman, recruiter, fire administration; Wanda Gurley-Jordon, volunteer, Phoebus Rescue Squad; Joe Howard, volunteer secretary, Phoebus Rescue Squad; and Chris Larson, captain, Phoebus Rescue Squad; front row, left to right: Jeffrey Smith and Patrick Goldschmidt, Hampton Volunteer Fire Company Firefighters; and Peter Kalil, volunteer emergency medical technician, Wythe Rescue Squad (Daily Press/Buddy Norris).

UUUUUUU - Phoebus firefighters Bill Selby (second from left), George Selby, and Ernest Hale cool off after fighting a fire at Fort Monroe in 1986 (Hampton City Fire Dept. - Personnel Training).

Cutbacks and Jim Peach Saves the Day

By 1992 Hampton had budget difficulties and some hard decisions to make. For the Phoebus Fire Company, it meant reducing the number of firefighters at the Phoebus station from four career employees per shift to three. A lieutenant at the Phoebus fire station found himself alone to battle a stubborn fire 1 1/2 blocks away on a Friday morning in 1993, and Jim Peach would become the hero that Phoebus needed.

When the fire at 110 E. County St. was reported at 8:55am on March 19, 1993, Lt. Steve Seals was alone at the station. The other two firefighters had gone on an ambulance call outside Langley Air Force Base where a baby was having breathing problems. The burning structure was a garage in which a homeless man had been living with a heater, bed, table and other furnishings. The homeless man staggered from the burning building and was not injured.

"Jim Peach, owner of Peach's Texaco nearby on East Mellen Street, was in his parking lot when a woman in a red dress ran up to him screaming and pointing to smoke rising from a building. 'She shouted that there was a man in there,' Peach said. Peach said he climbed into his van and drove to the Phoebus Fire Station about 100 yards away. Peach then followed Seals to the fire. Peach had been hospitalized for chest pains the month before but was able to assist the officer by pulling fire hose from the engine. Shortly thereafter a firefighter who was off duty stopped to operate the pump while Seals changed into protective gear to fight the flames. The fire was out within 10 minutes.[259]

VVVVVVV - Jim Peach at his Texaco station in 1981 (Daily Press).

WWWWWWW - Lt. Steve Seals was the only firefighter at the Phoebus Fire Station when Jim Peach came knocking (Daily Press/Adrin Snider).

---

[259] David Chernicky, "Cutbacks Extinguish Workers" (*Daily Press*, March 20, 1993).

XXXXXXX - Lt. Steve Hensley cools down on the front steps of 215 Segar Street in 1985 (Hampton City Fire Dept. - Personnel Training).

Slaughter Lumber Fire 1995

YYYYYYY - Phoebus firefighters battle the R.F. Slaughter Lumber fire on the morning of April 13, 1995 (Tony Schmidt).

On April 12, 1995, Phoebus lost another institution when a monstrous fire ripped through the Slaughter Lumberyard at 50 North Mallory Street, destroying eight buildings, wiping out 85 percent of its inventory, and causing an estimated $400,000 in damage.[260]

"By daylight Wednesday, all that was left of the R.F. Slaughter Lumber Corp. was a heap, a mangled heap of ashes and twisted metal, piled high and scattered for most of a city block. A steady, black stream of warm water and charred debris flowed down North Mallory Street, carrying away small pieces of a Phoebus institution that had stood since 1908, down the sewers and out of sight."[261]

R.F. Slaughter was a native of New Kent County and settled in Phoebus in 1897. Slaughter was a contemporary of P.A. Fuller and he worked at Hampton Sash and Door Co. on Academy Street before starting the R.F. Slaughter Lumber Company at 50 N. Mallory St. in Phoebus in 1908.[262]

---

[260] Jeanne Peck, "Lumberyard Sale Draws Crowd" (*Daily Press*, June 23, 1995).
[261] David Chernicky and Blair Anthony Robertson, "Landmark Lumberyard in Ashes" (*Daily Press*, April 13, 1995).
[262] Jeanne Peck, "Lumberyard Sale Draws Crowd" (*Daily Press*, June 23, 1995).

"The lumberyard had survived and thrived through the decades, had weathered the lean times of the Depression, the rations of two world wars and the arrival, much later, of mammoth superstores. It even built coffins during the influenza epidemic of 1918 and 1919. But everyone knew it could not endure a fire. The fear of flames had always been there. For all those years, the mill stayed busy and the saws hummed all day."[263]

ZZZZZZZ - James Earl Brown rests in front of the remains of the R.F. Slaughter Lumber Corporation at 50 North Mallory Street on the morning of April 13, 1995 (Daily Press/Adrin Snider).

Through the years, R.F. Slaughter Lumber grew and prospered, and the lumberyard became "a legacy and a landmark. And for all those years, the fear was there, but the fire never came. At 1:15 a.m. Wednesday, it finally did, and there was nothing firefighters could do to stop the inferno. The flames roared 160 feet high as firefighters let loose with an onslaught of water from several angles. The water pummeling against the hot boards and sheet metal sent glowing embers flying over a two-block area. By 3 a.m., with the blaze under control but the yard's several buildings nearly all destroyed, thick clouds of gray smoke billowed toward the sky while William Charles, the company's owner, stood and watched. The cause of the fire remained a mystery Wednesday, but investigators had only begun to search through the huge pile of debris."[264]

---

[263] David Chernicky and Blair Anthony Robertson, "Landmark Lumberyard in Ashes" (*Daily Press*, April 13, 1995).
[264] Ibid.

AAAAAAAA - Slaughter Lumber in 1915 (Hampton Public Library).

BBBBBBBB - Slaughter Lumber owner William Charles, left, and his son, Adrian, watch the fire destroy their family business (Daily Press).

In the morning, everyone in Phoebus seemed to know what had happened and many came to "pay their respects, consoling employees, remembering earlier days and shaking their heads at the utter mess of it all."[265]

"'A fire of this magnitude,' said Battalion Chief Charles Davis, 'is very difficult to put out because the building more or less collapsed around us and now we have to pick that up and put out the fire beneath it.' One firefighter battling the blaze suffered smoke inhalation. He was treated at Sentara Hampton General Hospital and released."[266]

"The blaze was so hot that the heat cracked windshields on three fire trucks and melted a metal display plate on at least one of the engines. Two ladder trucks and five engines responded to the two-alarm fire. The blaze destroyed nearby telephone lines and knocked out service for 1,200 customers in the area, said John Friesz, from Bell Atlantic.
Tony Schmidt, grandson of Chief A.A. Schmidt, and a battalion chief was called to battle the blaze. Schmidt had worked at the lumberyard 25 years earlier. Now he was watching the end of a legacy as the fire burned out of control. "It has to go down as one of the biggest," he said, standing in the Farm Fresh [now Food Lion] parking lot across the street.[267]

"To the historians, this is a city landmark. It's been around for years. They've been fortunate to survive with the big companies like the HQs and Builders Squares. But it's harder for them because they've got to keep up with the prices. But, you got to hand it to them, they've been around a long time," said Schmidt.[268] The fire was ruled an accident.[269]

[265] David Chernicky and Blair Anthony Robertson, "Landmark Lumberyard in Ashes" (*Daily Press*, April 13, 1995).
[266] Ibid.
[267] Ibid.
[268] Ibid.
[269] Jeanne Peck, "Lumberyard Sale Draws Crowd" (*Daily Press*, June 23, 1995).

CCCCCCCC - Tidewater Regional Arson Panel Investigator Bruce Sterlin from the Portsmouth Fire Department walks over debris looking for clues to what started the lumberyard blaze (Daily Press/Billy Garrett).

Renovations at the Fire Station

By the late 1990s, the Phoebus Fire House was starting to show its age. The tower housing the bell, the huge fire siren, and the smaller ambulance siren were removed from the roof of the building in 2000. The siren had been silenced previously due to concerns that the vibrations were compromising the structural integrity of the brick mortar. The house siren was last sounded at midnight on New Year's Eve 2000 ushering in the new millennium.[270] An article in the Daily Press highlighted the challenges that the firefighters were facing as the building began a $150,000 renovation to upgrade the roof, windows and electrical system.

---

[270] "History of the Phoebus Volunteer Fire Department," *Phoebus Volunteer Fire Department* (2019), 5.

Firehouse long neglected

Phoebus station a source of pride

By Fred Tannenbaum
Daily Press

HAMPTON

Hampton Fire Capt. Bettie Reeves-Nobie's glimmering black uniform shoes made a scuffing sound climbing the linoleum stairway of the Phoebus fire station

Reaching the top and making two right turns, Reeves-Noble, who commands the station, stood inside the bunk room. Full-time firefighters and medics sleep there — when it's dry.

The single beds and lockers were covered with clear plastic. The once-white ceiling tiles featured irregularly shaped brown rings from water stains. Even though it was after 10 a.m., the room looked dark. Part of that was due to the wood paneling firefighters installed themselves some time ago. But it also was because only about half of the fluorescent light fixtures were

TODAY.
Fire and Rescue workers Francis Cook Jr., left, and Tim Pais raise the flag in front of the Phoebus fire station in December.

Kyndall Harkness
Daily Press

on. A handwritten card taped near the light switch gave a clue:
"Do not use light," was written in

Please see **Station/C2**

DDDDDDDD - Headline from that start of renovations on January 13, 2000 (Daily Press).

"Bettie Reeves-Nobles' glimmering black uniform shoes made a scuffing sound climbing the linoleum stairway of the Phoebus fire station. Reaching the top and making two right turns, Reeves-Nobles, who commands the station, stood inside the bunk room. Full-time firefighters and medics sleep there when it's dry. The single beds and lockers were covered with clear plastic. The once-white ceiling tiles featured irregularly shaped brown rings from water stains. Even though it was after 10 a.m., the room looked dark. Part of that was due to the wood paneling firefighters installed themselves some time ago. But it also was because only about half of the fluorescent light fixtures were on. A handwritten card taped near the light switch gave a clue: 'Do not use light' was written in marker. 'Water in light fixture.'"[271]

"The Phoebus firehouse, on Hope Street, is a handsome two-story sentinel dating back to when Phoebus was a self-governing fishing village. It's still a focal point of the neighborhood. It's still a source of pride among generations of volunteer firefighters who've protected the community for more than 100 years. Full-time firefighters have served here for almost 50 years. But the station has seen better days. Roof leaks have gone unrepaired for years. They have soaked the firefighters' beds on rainy nights. They have caused the walls in the French window alcoves to dissolve in places and

---

[271] Fred Tannenbaum, "Firehouse long neglected" (*Daily Press*, January 13, 2000).

182

look like thick suds in a dish sink. They have wreaked havoc with the electrical system. A nearly $150,000 renovation began in December. Roof work is expected to cost $91,000; electrical repairs, $16,000; and window replacement, $40,000.'"[272]

"'We can't wait for it to get done,' Reeves-Nobles said. 'But we'll believe it when we see it.' Following not too far behind Reeves-Nobles on the tour was Hampton Fire Chief Robert Green, who grew up next to the station and started his career here, and Phoebus Volunteer Fire Company Chief Leonard Sulzberger, who first joined in the 1960s."[273]

"Hampton City Councilman Tom Gear also followed along, leering and shaking his head at the deterioration he saw. Even though the work has started, Gear is appalled by the conditions the city is asking Phoebus firefighters to live in. He wants to make sure the work gets done right and soon. 'I'm not asking for a new station,' Gear said outside the bunk room. 'I'm asking for it to be maintained. There's no excuse for allowing staff to live like this,' he said. 'When we put all our money into renovating downtown, we let our infrastructure go.'"[274]

EEEEEEEE - Hampton City Councilman Tom Gear looks out the window at standing water

---

[272] Fred Tannenbaum, "Firehouse long neglected" (*Daily Press*, January 13, 2000).
[273] Ibid.
[274] Ibid.

on the lower roof of the Phoebus fire station (Daily Press/Kyndell Harkness).

"Chief Green said he didn't know the exact reason why fire station maintenance was put off so long. He stood in the firefighters' day room, a place where firefighters can relax or study in between calls or performing daily maintenance or housekeeping chores. There's a television mounted on a high shelf in the corner with a plastic bowl on top of it to shield it from water. The city experienced some lean budget years in the past, Green said, so money was needed elsewhere. He regretted that the window repairs probably would mean the multi-paned French windows would be replaced."[275]

"The station was dedicated in 1938, during the Depression's twilight. In fact the station was part of Phoebus' City Hall, complete with offices, council chambers, a courtroom, police station and jail. All the rooms are now adapted to fire department uses. Some things have changed: The arch separating two truck bays was removed to fit larger rigs. Other things haven't: The fire station still is a community social center. Two wood-and-metal benches line the ramp leading from the bays. Their fresh tan paint still gleams. The benches invite fire crews to relax outside or neighbors to visit on warm days or nights."[276]

"There will be another casualty from the work. The station's roof-mounted siren and bell are coming down. They once summoned volunteers to their duty. Radio pagers have replaced them. The siren was last blown as a farewell salute during the August 1998 funeral of former volunteer Chief George Selby Sr., who served the volunteer fire company for six decades. Veteran volunteer firefighter Ray Mingee, who joined while in high school, came up the stairs to the day room. He explained that the siren blew three times to summon volunteers for an ambulance run and up to six times for a fire call, telling volunteers which of Phoebus' six wards or districts to go to. 'The siren also would blow at noon,' Mingee said, 'and like heck at New Year's.' The bell was used during World War II, when using a siren would have panicked the community into thinking an air raid was imminent."

"Regardless of how firefighters were summoned, two trucks would leave the station. Veterans said the first would head directly to the fire. The second would head up Mellen Street picking up business owners who dropped everything to serve their town. Mingee and volunteer Chief Sulzberger returned to the volunteer dining room in the old jail after Chief

---

[275] Fred Tannenbaum, "Firehouse long neglected" (*Daily Press*, January 13, 2000).
[276] Ibid.

Green and Capt. Reeves-Nobles returned to other duties and Gear returned to work. They drank steaming coffee from foam cups and discussed the fire department's place in the community. The paid firefighters prepare meals for homeless people each Sunday at Zion Baptist Church. Volunteer firefighters have a partnership with Mouton and Bryan schools. They also hand out candy during the annual Phoebus Christmas parade. Generations of families have served as volunteers. Fuller, Sulzberger, Kearney and Mugler are just a few of the family names. 'It was the thing to do,' said Mingee, who started as a 'lantern boy,' responsible for lighting the lamps that once hung off the sides of the old firetrucks. 'It was the social organization of the community. Any and everybody socially belonged to the fire department.'[277]

FFFFFFFF - The Phoebus Volunteer Fire Company sponsored the Fourth Annual Fire Prevention Poster Contest winners in 2002. All students who participated were from Phoebus. Back row, left to right, Leonard P. Sulzberger, Phoebus Volunteer Fire Company Chief; Ernest L. Hale, Phoebus Volunteer Fire Company President, and Hampton Mayor Mamie Locke. Front row, from left to right: Tevin Brown, Tierra Dorsey, Takerra Andrews, Latise Turner and Jordan Shuck.

"Medic-firefighter Francis Cook Jr. said firefighters stationed in Phoebus and neighborhood residents get to know one another and bond. That's what he said brought him back to the station after serving in some of Hampton's other stations for more than three years. 'I did everything I could to get back here,' Cook said. He sat in an upstairs office, with a wheelbarrow and welders' gas cylinders on a cart visible out the window on

---

[277] Fred Tannenbaum, "Firehouse long neglected" (*Daily Press*, January 13, 2000).

the roof. 'Everybody's got their own house they want to go back to. I like it here. Our house may be old, but it's home,' Cook said. 'We live in it work in it try to keep her up as best we can. She needs a little help, and she's starting to get it."[278]

GGGGGGGG - Sam's Restaurant burns on Christmas Day in 2005. It had been damaged in Hurricane Isabel (Daily Press).

HHHHHHHH - Steve Sanzo, Ronnie Collins, and John Cizmar putting wreaths on the graves of Phoebus firefighters on Memorial Day 2019 (Paul Sulzberger).

---

[278] Fred Tannenbaum, "Firehouse long neglected" (*Daily Press*, January 13, 2000).

Pride of Phoebus Spotlight
E.L. "Bubba" Hale
Battalion Chief
First recipient of the Hampton Firefighters' Medal of
Valor in 1956
Life: 1927-2018

Ernest L. Hale was born at Fort Monroe in 1927 and he spent the
majority of his life in the Phoebus area. Starting at the young age of
sixteen his passion for firefighting led him to be a lantern boy for the
Phoebus Fire Company.

A World War II veteran of the Pacific Theater, he enlisted at the young
age of seventeen and spent four years in service as a firefighter in the
U.S. Navy. Upon returning to Hampton, Bubba began his thirty-eight-
year career with the Hampton Fire Department, rising to the rank of
Battalion Chief.

Hale received the first Hampton Firefighters' Medal of Valor in 1956.
Hale also famously captured a bull that escaped a rodeo at the Hampton
Coliseum and charged down Pembroke Avenue.

IIIIIII - Hale in the late 1980s (Pam Hale Johnson).

11 LADIES' AUXILIARY

The Phoebus Fire Company Ladies' Auxiliary was organized after consolidation in November 1952 and consisted of forty charter members. They formed primarily to provide support to the Virginia State Firemen's Convention that was coming to Phoebus in 1953.[279]

The organization's main objective was "to aid the Fire Company in every way possible to foster its every cause and to stand behind them in everything they undertake any assistance we can at all times," according to a write-up in the 1963 Firemen's Convention book.

In practice this would be making meals and providing hot coffee during fires or when the firefighters returned.[280] In 1953, the Phoebus Ladies' Auxiliary included officers Mrs. Carl A. Hellman, Jr. Mrs. Guy Mugler, and Mrs. Harrison Hill along with Winifred Newcomb, Virginia Johnson, Virginia Barnett, Mary S. Carroll, Rose Cooper, Dorothy G. Craigs, Bernice F. Fetters. Elizabeth A. Ferber, Jean M. Galla, Dorothy L. Goodrich. Catherine A. Hunt. Odie N. Johnson, Mildred L. Kaiser, Ellen Kuss, Mary M. Luther, Mattie M. Mittlemaier, Vige Monta, Marie Nicoletta. Frances Roach. Ida H. Routten. Rose Saunders, Eleanor M. Selby, Kathleen M. Snow, Lois P. Spriggs. Eva M. Stinson, Catherine S. Tyler, Mattie L. Warren, Cecil Welch, A. T. Wells. Effie F. Wilder, Emily H. Zephir and Mary D Johnston.[281]

The women would work on community issues of the day like contributing to countless community events and raising funds for new uniforms for the Fire Company and new equipment like a ambulance for the First Aid Rescue Squad in 1954. They would even lead fundraisers that contributed to eradicating polio after Jonas Salk discovered the vaccine in 1952.

---

[279] "Phoebus Auxiliary Schedules Second Planning Meeting," *Daily Press* (September 30, 1952).
[280] "Phoebus, Buckroe, Firemen Note Auxiliary Activities," *Daily Press* (April 19, 1953).
[281] Ibid.

PHOEBUS FIRE AUXILIARY GIVES CHECK FOR AMBULANCE

JJJJJJJ - Mrs. Carl A. Hellman, president of the Ladies' Auxiliary, presents a check to John P. Mugler, treasurer of the First Aid Squad of the Phoebus Fire Company, for the $1,170 for a new ambulance in 1954. In the group at the presentation were (left to right) Mrs. Harrison P. Hill, president-elect; Mrs. Hellman; Miss Mabel Hurley, secretary-elect; Mrs. R. F. Snow, vice president-elect; and Mugler (Daily Press).

They would also travel with the Phoebus Fire Company to participate in events and parades. The Phoebus Fire Auxiliary Marching Unit was a 17-member marching unit of the Ladies Auxiliary of the Phoebus Fire Company, the first in the Tidewater District. According to an article from 1955, the marching unit would wear uniforms with a navy-blue skirt, white blouse, gold tie and navy-blue cap. They carried a swagger stick decorated with blue and gold ribbons and wear white gloves and black shoes.[282]

In the photo below, the women take a photo before traveling to Staunton to march in the annual State convention in 1955.

---

[282] "17 in Phoebus Auxiliary Leave for Convention," *Daily Press* (August 7, 1955).

KKKKKKKK - The Phoebus Fire Company Ladies' Auxiliary Marching Unit in August 1955. In the photo (left to right) are Mrs. Robert Snow Jr., auxiliary vice president; Mrs. Carl Hellman, Jr., past president; Mrs. Harrison Hill, president, and Miss Mabel Hurley, secretary (Daily Press).

LLLLLLLL – Banner Girls from the Ladies' Auxiliary - Left to right: June Galla, Sandra Antill, Pat Wilkinson, and Barbara Small (Paul Sulzberger).

MMMMMMMM - Officers of the Phoebus Fire Companies Ladies' Auxiliary in 1963. Seated, left to right: Mrs. William Smith, President; Mrs. George Selby, Vice President; Mrs. Stephen Galla, Treasurer; Mrs. Raymond Selby, Corresponding Secretary; Mrs. Viola Ross, Secretary. Stand, left to right: Mrs. Herbert Luther, Assistant Conductress; Mrs. Albert Mittlemaier, Conductress; Mrs. Bernard Stinson, Historian; Mrs. Robert Snow, Parliamentarian, Mrs. Malcolm Alligood, Drill Captain (Martha Morris).

NNNNNNNN - Officers and members of the Phoebus Fire Company Ladies' Auxiliary. Front row, left to right: Bessie Smith, Janet Selby, Jean Galla, Peggy Selby, Viola Ross. Second row, left to right: Mattie Warren, Helen Hill, Sandra Antill, Nancy Luther, Pat Wilkinson, Gail Stattler, Kathleen Snow, Dot Goodrich, Frances Stony. Back row, left to right: Edie Hillman, Lucy Mae Hill, Mattie Mittlemaier, Eva Stinson, Grace Alligood, Dot Wilkinson, Barbara Small, June Galla (Martha Morris).

OOOOOOOO - Wallace Hicks, of the Virginia State Firemen's Association, meets with officers of Phoebus Fire Company Auxiliary on November 29, 1963. Front row, left to right: Mrs. William R. Smith, president; Mrs. George Selby, vice-presidents; Miss Gayle Stofler, secretary; Mrs. Stephen Galla, treasurer. Back row, left to right: Mrs. Malcolm Alligood, drill sergeant; Mrs. Robert Snow, parliamentarian; Mrs. Carl Hellman, chaplain (Daily Press).

PPPPPPPP - Ladies Auxiliary - Phoebus Fire Department. (Jean Galla).

Phoebus Auxiliary

The Ladies Auxiliary to The Phoebus Fire Company, will hold its annual installation banquet on Saturday at 6:30 p.m. at the Civilian Club, Ft. Monroe.

Emil Sulzburger, a local attorney, will be guest speaker and will also install the following officers for 1972-73: Mrs. Galen Ross, president; Mrs. Jack Wilkinson, vice president; Mrs. Frank Leviner, recording secretary; Mrs. Tommy Mugler, corresponding secretary; Mrs. Stephen Galla, treasurer; Mrs. Tony Sanzo, chaplain; Mrs. Berthamae Pearce, conductress; Mrs. Cecil Wyatt, assistant conductress; Mrs. Henry Beimler, drill captain; Mrs. William Smith, assistant drill captain; and Mrs. B. G. Odom, historian.

The auxiliary will also be celebrating its 20th anniversary.

QQQQQQQQ - 20th anniversary on November 12, 1972.

RRRRRRRR - Connie Clarke's ribbon from the 1955 Virginia State Firemen's Association convention (Tom Jackson).

SSSSSSSS - Madeline Stowell Sanzo and Evelyn Stowell Dawson in their Phoebus Fire Department Auxiliary uniforms. The sisters had just participated in a Phoebus Day parade (Pam Sanzo).

ABOUT THE AUTHORS

Tim Receveur

Tim Receveur is a director at PeaceTech Lab in Washington, D.C., a non-profit organization that explores ways to use technology to reduce violent conflict around the world. Tim is an Air Force veteran and spent 13 years at the U.S. Department of State working on applied technology. Tim now lives in Phoebus with his wife, April, and dog, Puzzles.

Tim runs the daily blog *Phoebus and Fort Monroe: Then and Now* on Facebook and Instagram. He also runs a website called *Phoebus Memories* (phoebusmemories.org), dedicated to cataloging photos and stories from Phoebus.

Tom Jackson

Dr. Thomas L. Jackson is a Research Professor in the Department of Mechanical and Aerospace Engineering and Technical Manager for the Center for Compressible Multiphase Turbulence, all at the University of Florida. Born and raised in Hampton, he is a descendant of Henry and Elizabeth Lancer of Phoebus. Tom lives with his wife, Norma, in Gainesville, Florida.

BIBLIOGRAPHY

"13 Men Qualify As First Aid Instructors," *Daily Press* (November 16, 1947).

"17 in Phoebus Auxiliary Leave for Convention," *Daily Press* (August 7, 1955).

"3-Day Convention of State Firemen Opens in Phoebus," *Daily Press* (August 28, 1930).

"A Disgraceful Riot," *Alexandria Gazette* (June 15, 1898).

"A Drive at Phoebus," *Daily Press* (June 12, 1898).

"A Great Success," *Phoebus Sentinel* (May 20, 1905).

"A Riot in Phoebus," *Daily Press* (August 23, 1898).

"Alleged 'Fire Bugs' Get Scotch Verdict," *Daily Press* (December 21, 1905).

"Ambulance Men Put Out Blaze," *Daily Press* (November 10, 1949).

"Big Fire in Phoebus," *Daily Press* (March 26, 1898).

"Business Block in Phoebus Threatened," *Daily Press* (December 17, 1909).

"Closes Tonight," *Daily Press* (May 16, 1905).

"Council of NN Commends the Life of Late Mayor Snow," *Daily Press* (October 15, 1948).

"Delegates Leave Tonight," *Daily Press* (August 23, 1910).

"Details are Arranged for Firemen's Parade," *Daily Press* (August 28, 1930).

"Disorderly Proceedings," *Alexandria Gazette* (August 22, 1898).

"Entire Tank Farm May Be Doomed," *Daily Press* (April 25, 1958).

"Famous Resort," *Daily Press* (March 8, 1920).

"Fire Alarms Protect Historic Sites," *Daily Press* (July 25, 1985).

"Fire Department of Phoebus is the Pride of the Town," *Daily Press* (January 25, 1920).

"Fire Fiend Scared the Town," *Daily Press* (December 19, 1905).

"Fire in Phoebus," *Daily Press* (January 21, 1904).

"Firemen Begin Week-Long Conclave in Phoebus Area," *Daily Press* (August 10, 1953).

"Fireman Davis Hurt," *Daily Press* (May 10, 1905).

"Firemen Drill in Public," *Phoebus Sentinel* (September 2, 1905).

"Firemen, Legion to Place Flowers on Graves Today," *Daily Press* (May 30, 1938).

"Firemen's Fair in Phoebus is Opened," *Daily Press* (May 1, 1923).

"Forty-First Convention Virginia Firemen to Open in Phoebus Today," *Daily Press* (August 27, 1930).

"Frank A. Kearney Dies in Phoebus from Influenza," *Daily Press* (October 24, 1918).

"Full-Time Firemen and Insurance Rates," *Daily Press* (December 13, 1954).

"Historic Romance of the Chamberlin," *Daily Press* (March 9, 1920).

"Hotel Chamberlin Destroyed By Flames," *Daily Press* (March 8, 1920).

"History of the Phoebus Volunteer Fire Department" *Phoebus Volunteer Fire Department* (2019), 3.

"Impressive Rites Feature Laying of 2 Cornerstones," *Daily Press* (November 16, 1938).

"In a Blaze of Glory," *The Norfolk Virginian* (April 5, 1896).

"It Shines Like $12,300," *Daily Press* (January 14, 1951).

"It's All Yours Mayor," *Daily Press* (January 14, 1951).

"Look back: Esso Standard Oil Company Fire," *Daily Press* (April 15, 2018).

"Mrs. Kenyon Buys Roseland, Paying $125,000 for It," *Daily Press* (July 22, 1919).

"Needed Improvements Planned for Phoebus," *Daily Press* (June 8, 1906).

"New Fire Engine Arrives For Use By Town Firemen," *Daily Press* (May 12, 1940).

"New Motor Tractor for Phoebus Arrives," *Daily Press* (October 16, 1916).

"New Town Fire Department Culminates Dream Fostered 40 Years Ago in Phoebus," *Daily Press* (November 20, 1938).

"Now in Full Blast," *Daily Press* (May 11, 1905).

"Oldest Volunteer in Parade Today," *Daily Press* (August 17, 1956).

"Our Guests, The Virginia Firemen," *Mount Carmel Item* (October 7, 1908).

"Quiet Restored," *The Times (Richmond)* (August 23, 1898).

"Phoebus Auxiliary Schedules Second Planning Meeting," *Daily Press* (September 30, 1952).

"Peninsula Extension," *Wikipedia* (March 21, 2018), https://en.wikipedia.org/wiki/Peninsula_Extension.

"Phoebus All Right," *Daily Press* (August 15, 1899).

"Phoebus, Buckroe, Firemen Note Auxiliary Activities," *Daily Press* (April 19, 1953).

"Phoebus' Big Blaze," Phoebus Sentinel (November 11, 1905).

"Phoebus Fire Boys Get 200 Calls in '45," *Daily Press* (January 6, 1946).

"Phoebus Fire Co. Trophies Unusual," *Daily Press* (December 8, 1964).

"Phoebus Fire Department Observes 50th Anniversary," *Daily Press* (January

14, 1943).

"Phoebus Fire Dept. Had 741 Calls in '51, Chief Reports," *Daily Press* (January 13, 1952).

"Phoebus Firemen Get Royal Welcome Home Last Night," *Daily Press* (August 24, 1924).

"Phoebus Firemen To Give Benefit Dance in Armory," *Daily Press* (January 26, 1938).

"Phoebus Great Showing," *Daily Press* (August 27, 1909).

"Phoebus Infected," *Daily Press* (August 2, 1899).

"Phoebus Ladies Meet Thursday," *Daily Press* (Mach 23, 1927).

"Phoebus Men Are Thanked for Fight," *Daily Press* (March 19, 1920).

"Phoebus Sewer System," *Richmond Dispatch* (April 25, 1902).

"Phoebus Town Has Big Blaze," *Daily Press* (November 5, 1905).

"Phoebus Volunteers Began Fire Fighting Unit in '93," *Daily Press* (July 12, 1953).

"Rescue Squad," *Daily Press* (August 9, 2012).

"Riot At Phoebus," *Daily Press* (October 19, 1898).

"Roseland Manor," *Daily Press* (December 29, 1985).

"Schmidt is Chief Phoebus Firemen for Coming Year," *Daily Press* (January 13, 1931).

"Social, Business Events Scheduled As Hampton Set to Welcome 2,000 Firemen," *Daily Press* (August 9, 1953).

"Special Fund to Pay for Ambulance," *Daily Press* (October 13, 1947).

"Special Grand Jury," *Alexandria Gazette* (November 11, 1898).

"Stories of John Chamberlin," *The Liberty Vindicator (Liberty, Texas)* (July 23,

1897).

"The Conflagration at Hampton," *The Staunton Spectator* (April 15, 1884).

"The Fire in Phoebus," *The Times (Richmond, Virginia)* (January 21, 1893).

"The Lamp Exploded," *Daily Press* (September 28, 1898).

"The Reform Ball Rolling," *Daily Press* (April 1, 1902).

"The New Town Councilmen," *Phoebus Sentinel* (July 6, 1901).

"To Be Continued," *Daily Press* (May 14, 1905).

"To The Voters of Phoebus, VA," *Daily Press* (August 11, 1938).

"Trouble Seems to Be Over," *Daily Press* (August 25, 1898).

"Tucker in Hampton," *Daily Press* (August 24, 1898).

"Tyler in Phoebus," *Daily Press* (April 3, 1900).

"Virginia Bills," *The Times (Richmond)* (December 12, 1901).

"Virginia News," *Peninsula Enterprise* (October 22, 1898).

"Volunteer and Paid Firemen Feuding," *The Danville Register* (October 13, 1977).

"Will Have Fountain," *Daily Press* (July 21, 1905).

"William H. Trusty House," United States Department of the Interior (United States: June 22, 1979), https://www.dhr.virginia.gov/VLR_to_transfer/PDFNoms/114-0108_WillamHTrustyHouse_1979_Final_Nomination.pdf.

"Work on City Halls in Hampton, Phoebus Progresses," *Daily Press* (October 2, 1938).

"Works Progress Administration (WPA)," *History* (A&E Television Networks: August 21, 2018), https://www.history.com/topics/great-depression/works-progress-administration.

"York Firemen Take the Town of Phoebus," *Daily Press* (October 20, 1910).

Adrian Miller, *The President's Kitchen Cabinet: The Story of the African Americans Who Have Fed Our First Families, from the Washingtons to the Obamas* (Chapel Hill, NC: University of North Carolina Press, 2017), 98.

Al Christopher, "Fire Department Organization Given Close Scrutiny" (*Daily Press*, November 8, 1975).

Anne W. Chapman, "Fight For Home Saves Plantation," *Daily Press* (August 11, 1991).

Annie C. Newsome, "The Phoebus Story - Past and Present," *Daily Press* (December 7, 1969).

Betsy Edison, "When Fire Sire Sounds, Junior Volunteers Answer Alarm" (*Daily Press*, June 23, 1963).

Dave Schleck, "Phoebus United Methodist Began As A 'Yankee Church'," *Daily Press* (December 8, 1995).

David Chernicky, "Cutbacks Extinguish Workers" (*Daily Press*, March 20, 1993).

David Chernicky, "Hampton Fire Training Program Becoming a Hot Potato" (*Daily Press*, November 20, 1980).

David Chernicky, "Volunteers Battle Fire Chief's Plans," *Daily Press* (June 5, 1989).

David Chernicky and Blair Anthony Robertson, "Landmark Lumberyard in Ashes" (*Daily Press*, April 13, 1995).

Deborah Hyman, "A Firefighting Century in Phoebus" (*Daily Press*, July 29, 1993).

Dick Solito, "Phoebus, ECC and Hampton to Consolidate," *Daily Press* (June 18, 1982).

Fred Tannenbaum, "Firehouse long neglected" (*Daily Press*, January 13, 2000).

Jane Keane Polonsky and Joan McFarland Drum, *Hampton's Haunted Houses*

& How to Feed a Ghost (Hampton, VA: Affordable Printing & Copies, Inc., 1998), 38.

Jeanne Peck, "Lumberyard Sale Draws Crowd" (*Daily Press*, June 23, 1995).

Jim Wright, "Phoebus Keeps Best of Past with Today's Changes," *Daily Press* (October 14, 1979).

John V. Quarstein (historian, *Big Bethel: The First Battle*), conversation with author, January 9, 2019.

Lynda R. Page, "Manor house gutted," *Daily Press* (April 1, 1985).

Mark St. John Erickson, "Hotel Chamberlin boosted Hampton resort's status" (Daily Press, March 8, 2018).

Mark St. John Erickson, "Landmark Chamberlin Hotel burns in March 1920 fire" (Daily Press, March 13, 2014).

Parke Rouse, Jr, *The Good Old Days in Hampton and Newport News* (USA: Dietz Press, 1986), 67.

Parke Rouse, "Prohibition, Consolidation Unable to Conquer Phoebus," *Daily Press* (February 12, 1995), https://www.dailypress.com/news/dp-xpm-19950212-1995-02-12-9502100251-story.html.

Robert Graves, "Consolidated Hampton Turns 30 Today," *Daily Press* (July 1, 1982).

Letter from George H. Lancer, (December 6, 1930).

Official Program for Dedication of Phoebus (April 2, 1900).

Phoebus Fire Department Meeting Minutes, (January 25, 1893).

Phoebus Fire Department Meeting Minutes, (January 30, 1893).

Phoebus Fire Department Meeting Minutes, (February 20, 1893).

Phoebus Fire Department Meeting Minutes, (April 13, 1893).

Phoebus Fire Department Meeting Minutes, (June 12, 1893).

Phoebus Fire Department Meeting Minutes, (July 17, 1893).

Phoebus Fire Department Meeting Minutes, (July 24, 1893).

Phoebus Fire Department Meeting Minutes, (July 31, 1893).

Phoebus Fire Department Meeting Minutes (August 3, 1896).

Phoebus Fire Department Meeting Minutes (September 7, 1896).

Phoebus Fire Department Meeting Minutes, (November 7, 1898).

Phoebus Fire Department Meeting Minutes, (January 2, 1899).

Town Council Meeting Notes (February 20, 1902).

Town Council Meeting Notes, (November 7, 1916).

Town Council Meeting Notes, (December 5, 1916).

Town Council Meeting Notes, (January 2, 1917).

Town Council Meeting Notes, (February 6, 1917).

Made in the
USA
Middletown, DE